SWEENEY TODD

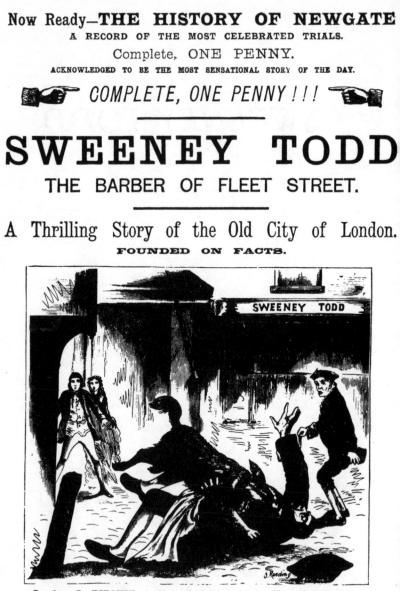

Now Ready—**THE HISTORY OF NEWGATE**

A RECORD OF THE MOST CELEBRATED TRIALS.

Complete, ONE PENNY.

ACKNOWLEDGED TO BE THE MOST SENSATIONAL STORY OF THE DAY.

COMPLETE, ONE PENNY ! ! !

SWEENEY TODD

THE BARBER OF FLEET STREET.

A Thrilling Story of the Old City of London.

FOUNDED ON FACTS.

London—A. RITCHIE, 6 & 7, Red Lion Court, Fleet Street, E.C.

A typical Victorian 'penny dreadful' about the Demon Barber published towards the end of the nineteenth century.

SWEENEY TODD

The Real Story of the
Demon Barber of Fleet Street

Peter Haining

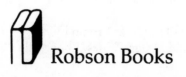 Robson Books

This paperback edition published in Great Britain in 1998 by Robson Books Ltd, Bolsover House, 5-6 Clipstone Street, London W1P 8LE

First published in hardback in 1993.

British Library Cataloguing in Publication Data
A catalogue record for this title is available from the British Library

ISBN 1 86105 163 8

Chair on p. 68 drawn by Jonathan Baker

Printed and bound in Great Britain by
Creative Print and Design Wales, Ebbw Vale

*This book is dedicated
to the memory of
TOD SLAUGHTER
'I'm polishing 'em off well tonight!'*

'Sweeney Todd will never die. We all need bogeymen and he was bogier than most.'

Anna Pavord, *Observer*, 29 January, 1979.

CONTENTS

PREFACE

In July 1980 when Stephen Sondheim's Emmy award-winning 'Musical Thriller', *Sweeney Todd*, opened in London, a considerable amount of the original research that I had gathered about the Demon Barber of Fleet Street was used as the basis for a TV Special on Melvyn Bragg's *South Bank Show* which discussed the making and shaping of the stage production. At the same time I was also asked to contribute an introduction to a new edition of one of the classic melodramas about the cut-throat barber written in 1862 by the Victorian playwright Frederick Hazelton.

There was still, at that time, a great deal of confusion and disagreement about Sweeney Todd, which I went to some lengths to describe. In particular, whether the man had really existed at all, or was simply the product of an author's fertile imagination. It was a question that had fascinated me for twenty years ever since my early career as a journalist employed in Fleet Street — and one that I was still very keen to answer.

As a result of my involvement in that television programme — which, incidentally, also won an Emmy award for London Weekend Television in the performing arts category — not to mention the re-publication of the Victorian melodrama, I received a number of interesting letters and communications from people similarly intrigued by the mystery surrounding the Demon Barber. These missives spoke of old manuscripts in the British Museum, documents held in the Guildhall in London, and a number of eighteenth- and nineteenth-century journals and newspapers on file in the British Library at Colindale. There were hints, too, that the Library of Congress in Washington D.C. also had some interesting data relating to Sweeney Todd.

Because of the pressure of other commitments, I was not free to follow all these leads immediately. But in the intervening years I have, one by one, followed up each of the suggestions — travelling to Washington as well as combing London in the search — and I have discovered new and invaluable information to supplement what was already in my possession. These clues pointed inescapably to the fact that Sweeney Todd *had* existed and that his life and crimes were more intriguing, more curious and, if anything, more gruesome than had previously been suspected.

It was certainly also impossible to escape from the conclusion that much of Sweeney Todd's notoriety had stemmed directly from a Victorian 'Penny Dreadful' serial which had subsequently been pirated for use in plays at the cheap London theatres during the closing years of Queen Victoria's reign. But equally certainly beneath this fiction there lay a substrata of fact that no amount of romanticising could hide. The belief expressed by some historians that the Demon Barber was a composite figure made from other serial killers was certainly tenable; but the facts that I came across in those manuscripts, documents and newspapers produced enough concrete evidence to enable me to recreate the life of this man whose cut-throat killings have caused him to be described as 'the greatest mass murderer in English history'.

It was a story made all the more fascinating because of two extraordinary elements unlike any others to be found in criminal history. Firstly, there was Sweeney Todd's use of a revolving shaving chair to trap his victims; and, secondly, the fact that he had a partner-in-crime, a woman, who helped in disposing of the bodies by turning the flesh into meat pies.

In writing this full story of Sweeney Todd, I have had access not only to all the evidence already mentioned, but in addition the opportunity to study the various well-known novelisations and serialisations of his life that have appeared over the years since the mid–1800s. From their pages I have similarly been able to sift more facts from amidst the fiction, with the result that while clearly separating one from the other, I am at last able to write what I believe is the real story of the Demon Barber.

The facts about Sweeney Todd's life are made all the more fascinating by what was happening in London during the later part of the eighteenth century: the depradation and poverty of the people; the general lawlessness, drunkenness and crime in which they lived; and the gradual emergence of acceptable working conditions, literacy and social order. These were the elements which initially enabled a mass killer like Todd to survive, but as they changed brought about his downfall. This is a story as much about society and its mores as the horrific crimes of one man.

At the end of my search for Sweeney Todd one question still remained to be answered. Why should we have been fascinated for so long by a man who was, to all intents and purposes, a callous murderer with no qualms about cannibalism? A forerunner, it would appear, to the cinema's number one human monster of the nineties, Hannibal Lector? The history books indicate that the public has always had a morbid interest in this theme, and psychologists have pointed out that one of mankind's most persistent subconscious fears is that of being killed and eaten. Sweeney Todd indeed epitomises that feeling one gets when eating a meat pie about just what *might* have gone into its manufacture; and the strange, tingling apprehension which creeps over anyone who leans back in a hairdresser's chair and waits for the razor or the scissors to be applied to the hairs on the neck or throat.

Reay Tannahill in her fascinating book, *Flesh and Blood: A History of the Cannibal Complex* (1975), says that many of the old beliefs about flesh, blood and the spirit are still buried somewhere in the recesses of our minds, but the public expression of them has become almost jaundiced. 'Except when it really happens,' she says, 'eating people is no longer startling or even very remarkable, just blackly humorous.' Miss Tannahill then goes on to cite a story which proves — if proof is needed — that the Sweeney Todd story will probably remain with us always. Apparently not very long ago there was a group of people in London distributing leaflets which warned against the activities of a 'world-wide neo-Nazi apparatus' which was said to be set on removing up to eight million British citizens. No reason was given for this or even how those who had been selected would be eliminated. Some of the victims, the leaflet declared, had already been disposed of and their bodies made into various innocuous items which had been slipped into the merchandising system. The items were leather goods, soap powder, fertiliser and — yes, you have already guessed — *meat pies*!

The public interest in the legend of Sweeney Todd seems to me never to have been in doubt. Perhaps the most unusual example of this happened only a short while ago in November 1991. A special production of Sondheim's musical was being mounted in Wormwood Scrubs, the London prison which houses a considerable number of murderers serving life sentences. Several of the inmates were playing roles in the musical, although the leading roles were being sung by professionals from the Pimlico Opera Company who had been invited to stage the production.

'What will people make of it?' one inmate was reported to have asked a member of the opera company. 'A bunch of murderers doing an opera about a bunch of murderers?' It was not a question that anyone felt qualified to answer. Indeed, probably only Sweeney Todd himself could have provided one. But then he would surely have found it the most curious twist of all in the legend which surrounds his name — that after all these years the story had finally came back full circle to prison where it had all begun.

1

The Legend of the Demon Barber

The name Sweeney Todd, the notorious Demon Barber of Fleet Street with his famous catch-phrase, 'I polish 'em off', is one of the most famous as well as enigmatic in the annals of crime. Renowned in folklore, sensational fiction, plays, films and, most recently, a lavish stage musical, he enjoys a world-wide notoriety as one of the earliest serial killers who perpetrated crimes that were as ingenious in their execution as they were ghoulish in their *modus operandi*.

His name is, in fact, one that hardly needs any introduction. To generations of children he has been held up as a razor-wielding bogeyman who would cut them up and make them into meat pies — long before Freddy Krueger became a nightmare in today's Elm Street movies, slashing children to death with razor-sharp fingers. To the older generation, Todd has also been regarded as a blood-soaked villain who cunningly used a revolving chair in his shop to tumble victims into a deep cellar below. Here, their throats were cut and any valuables removed, before the corpses were taken through underground passageways to his accomplice-in-crime, a pastrycook named Mrs Lovett, who turned them into pies for sale in her shop. The elements of cold-blooded murder and cannibalism made the story at once electrifying and appalling in the extreme.

These basic details of the story of Sweeney Todd are, in fact, as familiar in London lore as those of Jack the Ripper or Doctor Crippen; while his place in the history of crime in the city is as assured as that of Guy Fawkes or Dick Turpin. And although Fleet Street, where he carried out his hideous crimes in an

Sweeney Todd

unprepossessing little shop, has changed out of all recognition in the intervening two centuries since they were perpetrated, his ghost still haunts the former 'Street of Ink' and attracts curiosity seekers from all over the world. Unfortunately, no trace of that shop at 186 Fleet Street — or the other one occupied by Mrs Lovett in Bell Yard — still exists, but his reputation remains undiminished: if anything, it has become further enhanced. Indeed, in a grim little twist of fate, his name has even become synonymous in Cockney rhyming slang with those officers of the law bent on catching arch-criminals like him — the 'Sweeney' (Todd) or Flying Squad.

Yet for all his fame, the facts about Sweeney Todd's crimes remain remarkably poorly documented. Certainly, though, there are numerous references to him in case histories of crime as well as books about London.

In *The Crimes of London* by H. W. Maskell (1876), for instance, Todd is referred to as 'the most dastardly criminal of the age'. Maskell relates how when Todd was finally arrested, his premises were 'found crammed with property and clothing sufficient for 160 people'. *One hundred and sixty people!* — exaggerated or not, this total surely immediately places the Demon Barber among the forefront of the greatest mass-murderers in English history.

Charles Dickens, who began writing in the early part of the eighteenth century, certainly knew all about the Demon Barber and mentions him in Chapter 36 of his novel *Martin Chuzzlewit*, written in 1844.

' "Upon my word," thought Tom [Pinch], quickening his pace, "I don't know what John will think has become of me. He'll begin to be afraid I have strayed into one of those streets where the countrymen are murdered; and that I have been made meat pies of, or some such horrible thing." '

The theme also surfaces again in the next chapter:

'Tom's evil genius did not lead him into the dens of any of those preparers of cannibalistic pastry who are represented in many standard country legends as doing a lively retail business in the Metropolis.'

2

The villainous Sweeney Todd as portrayed in the 48-part serial published by Charles Fox in 1878.

Although these are clearly references to Sweeney Todd, Dickens may well have refrained from being more specific because of the possibility that some among his readers might have lost friends or relatives in the infamous barber's shop a little over forty years earlier.

William Kent in his interesting chronicle, *London Mystery and Mythology* (1952), mentions several old residents of the capital city who had told him stories about Sweeney Todd.

'Sir William Treloar, who was born over the famous carpet shop on Ludgate Hill, was familiar with the story of the Demon Barber and held it to be true. He also used to tell how, with a group of playfellows, he delighted in going into a barber's shop which stood at the corner of Fleet Street and Fetter Lane, with a doorway in each. At a concerted signal they would rush through the front door one after another and, shouting "Sweeney Todd" as they went, dash out of the Fetter Lane door. There was a rush as the last one ran a risk of being caught.'

Another writer, Clement Scott, a Victorian critic who was involved with the London theatre scene throughout the second half of the nineteenth century, adds to this statement in his memoirs, *The Drama of Yesterday* (1899):

'Old Temple Bar and its neighbourhood up to that day I always loved, although George Augustus Sala was forever telling us that the gate was not old at all. Within the fabric of Old Temple Bar was a tiny barber's shop where I have often been shaved. The Figaro who presided over the establishment delighted in tilting up the chair of his customers, and as the City boundaries came right through the shop he said, "Now you are in the West End — now you are in the City!" '

'I resented this joke, for I always thought of that grim drama by George Dibdin Pitt, first performed at the Brittania, Hoxton and called *Sweeney Todd, The Barber of Fleet Street; or The String of Pearls*. Sweeney Todd used to leave his customers sitting in the shaving chair on some paltry excuse, whereupon chair, customer and valuables disappeared through a trap to the cellar below, where the customer was robbed and promptly murdered.

I always connected that shop with Sweeney Todd; in fact I do so to this day.'

And just to underline these recollections, we have H. G. Hibbert, another historian of the stage, writing in his *A Playgoer's Memories* (1920):

'When I was a young Londoner I was shown in Fleet Street the very shop of the Demon Barber — and shuddered to think that meat pies were still on sale there. I read that an enterprising tradesman has again, by way of advertisement, labelled the new building erected on its site as the authentic abode of the wretch. I think it quite conceivable that there was a scoundrel, deep-dyed as the ghastly Todd, in the dark, Georgian days of London.'

In fact, all three of these writers were of the view that Sweeney Todd's shop had stood close to the Temple Bar. All had heard the stories, too, about a pie shop supposed to have existed in Bell Yard at this same point in history and perhaps linked to the barber's premises by interconnecting tunnels.

'There are plenty of underground apartments in Fleet Street,' William Kent added in his narrative. 'Beneath the Cheshire Cheese Tavern are vaults so extensive that they have been assigned by some to a religious priory.'

Another writer, Thomas Nelson, referring to Sweeney Todd by the nickname ascribed to him by Victorian Londoners as 'Old Cut 'em Up', said in his book, *Memories of Old London* (1904), that in the city the barber was held to be 'the worst of the worst' with a record of crimes 'unmatched for their cold-blooded, hardened and pitiless criminality'.

Alan Dent, until recently the distinguished theatre critic of the *Guardian*, and a man who had a particular interest in the stage melodramas about Sweeney Todd, had this to say in an article he wrote specially for *Lilliput* magazine in 1942: 'The legend has been in existence since the days of George II and the experts agree that it probably has a basis in fact. Fouche's *Archives of the Police* have an account of a similar series of murders in Paris, the victims being "polished off" in a barber's shop and then made into pies which were sold for human consumption.

'The Fleet Street tradition was in existence long before this, however. The late Chance Newton, who saw many of the early versions of the melodrama, investigated the matter carefully and came to the conclusion that Todd's shop was close to St Dunstan's-in-the-West at the highest point of Fleet Street. Until the year 1913 the site was occupied by Craig's celebrated fish restaurant. The sinister pie shop was situated in Bell Yard.

'Topographically, this is a little awkward, since it sets the barber's and the pie shop improbably far apart. However, the cellar where the chopping and baking were done was "of vast extent and sepulchral appearance". It must have extended right under Chancery Lane and what is now the Law Courts branch of the Bank of England.'

Alongside these references, however, there are others which assert that the man was nothing more than a figment of the imagination; that no such barber ever existed outside the pages of fiction or the repertory theatres. As recently as July 1980, the *Sunday Times* theatre critic Bevis Hillier completely refuted his predecessor's remarks by declaring, 'Almost certainly no demon barber called Sweeney Todd ever existed; but there is cut-throat competition over the identity of the real-life figure (or figures) on whom he was based.' (The careful use of the word 'almost' will probably strike the reader as strongly as it did me!)

In truth, the tale of the Demon Barber is one of the most bloodthirsty and intriguing to be found anywhere in the world, compounded by the lack of research and precious few documents on which to draw. It is a story that has fascinated me ever since the early days of my career in journalism when I worked for several years in Fleet Street at a time when it was still the newspaper centre of Britain.

Here, ostensibly just a stone's throw from the scene of his crimes, I kept running across versions of the Demon Barber's activities and conflicting stories about his reality. His name was one that cropped up with maddening frequency in discussions held in the Fleet Street pubs and was heard from tourists in the street asking for directions to 'where Sweeney Todd's shop was supposed to be'.

As a result I spent many fascinating hours walking the part of Fleet Street where he lived, visiting the shop at number 186 where he allegedly practised his barbering and cut his victims' throats (now completely rebuilt and occupied by an office equipment supplier), and strolling through quiet Bell Yard nearby, where Mrs Lovett's pie shop was said to be located.

I also examined the interior of the handsome St Dunstan's Church at the Strand end of Fleet Street, underneath which the passageway used for moving the corpses was said to run. I tried to picture in my mind's eye what the imposing gate of Temple Bar which had stood adjacent to the church looked like before it was removed and the spot marked by the present Griffin memorial. (This former 'Gateway to the City of London' was taken down over a century ago and relocated in Theobald's Park, Cheshunt, Hertfordshire, where it has been the subject of moves in recent years to be restored and returned to the capital once again.)

I pored over old records of Fleet Street and its inhabitants, looked at eighteenth-century maps for evidence of the actual premises used by Todd and Mrs Lovett, and carefully studied old engravings of the area in the hope I might spot a tiny shop bearing the legend, 'Sweeney Todd, Barber' or even just 'Barber'.

As time passed, the site took on the same sense of mystery for me that is associated with Whitechapel and the haunts of Jack the Ripper. Here was another area that was famous for a murderer both notorious and enigmatic. The similarities between the two men were curious, too: for just as the identity of Jack the Ripper has evaded the attentions of numerous writers and researchers, so Sweeney Todd has remained, through all the years since his death, a figure shrouded in conjecture. Both, though, have left their bloody and indelible mark across the fabric of London history.

As I walked through the area of Fleet Street on many a warm summer's day — and then again on dark winter evenings — the burning question of his reality kept returning to my thoughts. Every time I passed the Royal Courts of Justice I was reminded just how remarkable it was that such a legend could have grown

up in the very shadow of this great centre of British justice —
and yet there still remained in the minds of people this doubt as
to whether it had happened at all.

I was also surprised to find that for all his notoriety, there
was no full length biography of the Demon Barber. There had
been articles and features in magazines and newspapers, to be
sure; but, despite the continuing growth of his fame in all areas
of the media, the full story of Sweeney Todd still remained to
be written.

And so, over the intervening years, I have painstakingly
combed the fact and fiction to produce what I believe to be the
full story. I began, naturally enough, by looking at the earlier
accounts of murderous barbers which some believed might have
been the model for Sweeney Todd. They proved to be interesting,
if grisly, reading.

2

Who Was the Real Sweeney Todd?

The earliest of all the stories that have been claimed to be the inspiration for the legend of the Demon Barber of Fleet Street dates from as far back as the fifteenth century and takes the form of a medieval ballad written in French. The ballad was apparently sung by Parisian mothers as a warning to recalcitrant offspring. Later, it was adapted by folk singers and sung with relish to the tune of *Le Jeune Homme Emoisonne* — 'The Young Man Who Was Poisoned'. The words are as follows:

> *Towards the end of the Fourteenth Century*
> *There lived a sort of Demon Barber,*
> *Who slit his clients throats at 24 Rue des Marmouzets.*
>
> *He carried on this horrible trade*
> *And nobody could resist him,*
> *In his cellar he polished them off*
> *His accomplice a villainous pie merchant next door.*
>
> *CHORUS: With a pie — with a mer — with a chant,*
> *With a pie — mer — chant. Ha! Ha!*
>
> *This horrid tale also tells us*
> *That he worked with a ferocious female*
> *Fiercer than the fiercest bailiff.*
>
> *For all the poor devils he killed*
> *His partner converted into pork pies!*

> *And he said of his customers when defunct,*
> *They are gone — pork creatures!*
>
> *CHORUS: With a pork — with a cre — with a ture*
> *With a pork creature. Ha! Ha!.*

In a book of old French Ballads published in 1845 where I found a copy of these verses, the editor, M. Lurine, commented that 300 years later the story was still being told to young listeners — and for many of them 'nothing can wipe out the memory of the murderous pastrycook who served to frighten the little children of La Rue des Marmouzets.'

A second, and far more gruesome, contender as the role-model for Sweeney Todd appeared a hundred years later across the Channel in Scotland. Here, during the reign of James VI (later James I of England) a bloodthirsty young outcast named Sawney Beane started a reign of terror by preying on unsuspecting travellers in the Galloway area, first robbing and then killing his victims. What was more horrifying still was the fact that Beane then used the corpses to feed himself and his family.

There was no suggestion in the accounts about Sawney Beane that he was either a barber or turned his victims into meat pies, but there was evidence that he had been responsible for the death and cannibalism of about a thousand people during the space of twenty-five years. Not without good reason has he gone down in history as 'The Man Eater of Scotland'.

It seemed that Sawney lived with a woman of equally profligate and vicious ways in a remote cave near the coast of Galloway from which they operated — slaughtering anyone who came into the vicinity so there would be no witnesses to their crimes. And, a contemporary report goes on, 'being destitute of any means of obtaining food, the pair resolved to live on human flesh.

'Accordingly, when they had murdered any man, woman or child, they carried them to their den, quartered them, salted and pickled the members, and dried them for food. In this manner they lived, carrying on their depredations and murders until they had eight sons and six daughters, eighteen grandsons and four-teen granddaughters, all the offspring of incest.'

As the numbers of victims of Sawney Beane and his family mounted, so did the public outcry. The horror was intensified when a number of corpses, for which the killers obviously had no need, were discovered on the Galloway seashore. Finally, word was sent to Edinburgh and the authorities mounted a campaign of action.

Months of searching throughout Galloway failed to locate Sawney Beane — though several times groups of men passed the cave without realising anyone lived there. Finally, a party with bloodhounds, one of whom 'raised up an uncommon barking and noise' at the entrance to the cave, tracked the cannibals to their 'habitation of horrid cruelty'.

The hideaway proved to be about a mile in length and con-tained a network of passages and tunnels. The sights which confronted the members of the party who entered the gloomy, stench-ridden interior were almost beyond description, and made many of the men physically ill — as another account testifies:

'Legs, arms, thighs, hands and feet of men, women and children were suspended in rows like dried beef. Some limbs and other members were soaked in pickle; while a great mass of money, both of gold and silver, watches, rings, pistols, cloths, both woollen and linen, with an inconceivable quantity of other articles, were either thrown together in heaps or suspended on the sides of the cave.'

Not without difficulty, the wild family were rounded up. Then, after the human remains had been buried, the party returned to Edinburgh. A day later, Sawney Beane and his tribe were executed in Leith Walk without any formal trial, 'it being deemed unnecessary to try those who were avowed enemies to all mankind and of all social order,' the account says.

According to this same report, the manner of the death of Sawney Beane and his family was appropriate to the enormity of their crimes: the men all had their testicles and penises cut off, followed by their hands and legs, after which they were allowed to bleed slowly to death; the women, in the meantime, were made to watch the death of their menfolk and were afterwards all burned together on three huge bonfires.

Such is the story of Sawney Beane; and the connection between him and Sweeney Todd was first advanced in 1901 in the pages of the magazine, *Notes & Queries*, by a writer who signed himself, 'Gnomon'.

'I have always been under the impression,' 'Gnomon' wrote, 'that the legend of the Demon Barber of Fleet Street was suggested by the incidents of a *cause célèbre* in Scotland of the sixteenth century. This was the revolting trial of Sawney Beane and his associates transferred to London and Fleet Street where, to my personal knowledge, a penny pie-shop carried on its business in the forties of the last century on the very site attributed to it in the tale. Whether the adjacent house (at that date thriving as a cook-shop, conspicuous for that succulent kind of Yorkshire pudding described by Dickens in *David Copperfield* under the name of "spotted covey" from the raisins liberally adorning its greasy surface) was a barber's shop once I do not know.

'These two apparently very ancient houses stood about the centre of a group extending from the east corner of St Dunstan's Churchyard to the south-west corner of Fetter Lane. Many readers will remember them, for they were demolished but a very few years ago; their upper stories were of wood, and they were surmounted by a peculiar wood parapet or balustrade gallery overlooking the busy thoroughfare below. When the pie-shop discontinued purveying its special comestibles (and I have, as a boy, many times "sampled" its excellent wares), it was carried on as a bookseller's business under the conduct of a dealer of extremely peculiar views named Truelove, who also long ago disappeared.'

Of 'Gnomon' 's theory, I have to say that for a man who adopted a soubriquet meaning 'Indicator', I find the connection between the two killers tenuous in the extreme! The information he provides about the shops beside St Dunstan's is, however, a little more relevant to the real story of Sweeney Todd as we shall see later.

A century later, during the reign of Charles II (1630–1685), another series of events occurred which lead to the suggestion that Sweeney Todd might have been inspired not by a man, but by a similarly evil female barber! Women barbers were apparently fairly commonplace in London in the seventeenth century — several of them being based at Seven Dials.

This particular story is related by John Thomas Smith in his *Ancient Topgraphy of London* (1810). 'On one occasion,' he writes, 'that I might indulge the humour of being shaved by a woman, I repaired to the Seven Dials where, in Great St Andrew's Street, a slender female performed the operation, while her husband, a strapping soldier in the Horse Guards, sat smoking his pipe. There was a famous woman in Swallow Street who shaved, and I recollect a black woman in Butcher Row, a street formerly standing by the side of St Clement's Church, near Temple Bar, who is said to have shaved with dexterity.

'Mr Thomas Batrich, the entertaining and venerable barber of Drury Lane, informs me that he has read of the Barberess of Drury Lane who shamefully maltreated her customers in the reign of Charles the Second. It was said that this woman robbed her victims and when brought to trial her premises were found to be full of stolen goods. Mr Batrich made the sinister suggestion that she might have been the model for that story of the Demon Barber of Fleet Street.'

Again, this is not a suggestion I think we can take too seriously, although it is fascinating to learn of the existence of lady barbers who also nursed the same criminal intentions towards their unsuspecting customers.

In 1800 a French barber, or *peruquier,* was involved in some grisly acts of murder that marked him down as another suspect of the real Sweeney Todd. The man apparently carried out his profession in a 'long and dismal ancient street', the Rue-de-la-Harpe in the Faubourg St Marcell. For years he was regarded as a hard-working and conscientious barber, until word began to spread that a number of customers seen entering his shop were

The barber of the Rue de la Harpe *in Paris who was suspected of inspiring the Sweeney Todd legend.*

never seen to leave. Suspicions grew — and were then grue-somely confirmed when two friends from the provinces hap-pened to stop in the shop for a shave before continuing into the city to do some business. An account, translated from the French, which appeared in *The Tell Tale* magazine of 1825, informs us what happened next:

'These incautious travellers, whilst in the shop of this fiend, unhappily talked of the money they had about them. After being shaved, one of the men left on an errand and promised to return for his friend. The wretched barber, who was a robber and murderer by profession, as soon as the one turned his back, drew his razor across the throat of the other and plundered him.

'On his return, the other traveller was not content with the barber's explanation that his friend had left to find him. Getting no satisfaction from his enquiries, the traveller informed the authorities of his suspicions and they returned to the premises. There, despite the protestations of the *peruquier*, the premises were searched from top to bottom. The evidence of his crimes was found in every room.

'The remainder of the story is almost too horrible for human ears, but is not upon that account less credible. The barber was in partnership with a pastrycook in the Rue-de-la-Harpe whose shop was so remarkable for savory patties that they were sent for from the most distant parts of Paris. Those who were murdered by the razor of the one were concealed by the knife of the other in those very identical patties by which, independently of his partnership in those frequent robberies, he had made a fortune.

'This case was of so terrific a nature, it was made part of the sentence of the law, that besides the execution of the monsters upon the rack, the houses in which they perpetrated those infernal deeds should be pulled down, and that the spot on which they stood should be marked out to posterity with horror and execration.'

Tempting as it might be to see this account as the basis for the Sweeney Todd legend — if we were to accept him as fiction — there are several important reasons why this cannot be so. Firstly, it is most convenient that the shops where the murderous deeds were committed should have been raised to the ground so that no evidence remained. Secondly, there is no documentation in French criminal records of any such trial of a *peruquier* and a pastrycook in the year 1800. And, thirdly, the account in *The Tell Tale* appeared almost a quarter of a century *after* the events in London which were to bring Sweeney Todd to the gallows. If there is an explanation for this tale, surely, it is that the anonymous author plagiarised the events from their British setting and moved the story in its entirety to Paris. Xenophobia triumphs!

Two other sources of the story have also come to my notice. There is a German legend of a murderous barber operating in Cologne during the early years of the eighteenth century which, I would suggest, falls into the same category as the Rue-de-la-Harpe story; while in *Notes & Queries*, a reader named Alban Doran wrote in October 1878:

'Ten years ago I read in a French paper an incident which was said to have occurred in Morocco in the spring of the same year. But it was the tale of our old friend, Sweeney Todd. The same legend, hardly differing from the French version, is to be found in *Les Rues de Paris* published in 1844.'

Far from the Demon Barber having been modelled on the exploits of someone else, it seems clear to me that he was the original from whom others afterwards saw fit to borrow. Indeed, the real story of Sweeney Todd is, like much fact, far stranger than fiction; and, equally, more interesting and gruesome than any of these alleged prototypes.

3

The Road to Crime

Sweeney Todd was born on 26 October, 1756, in Brick Lane, Stepney. The actual house in which the child first breathed the fetid air of a London slum is not known, though it has been suggested it may have been one of a trio of three-storey buildings, numbers 85, 87 or 89, on the west side of the street, near the junction with Hanbury Street and just a stone's throw from Spitalfields Market.

According to the Royal Commission on Historical Monuments, carried out in 1930, the three tall properties, with their distinctive brick bands between the upper stories, had been in existence since the early eighteenth century, though by the middle of the century they were already showing signs of decay through overcrowding and neglect. It was in the attic of one of these that Sweeney Todd's mother, not yet twenty, gave birth to her son. She scratched a meagre living in winding silk. Her husband was a silk weaver.

The birth was not an easy one by all accounts, and Mrs Todd would have no more children. Her husband, because of the uncertain nature of his profession, had, like many of his fellows, already taken to heavy drinking and would consequently play little part in the rearing of his son. ('Gin', says historian David Hughson in his *History of London* [1806], 'was said to be the drink of the more sedentary trades, weavers particularly, and of women' — it was essentially a disease of poverty, so cheap, so warming and brought such forgetfulness of cold and misery.')

The omens for both the child and his parents were far from promising, although Sweeney Todd was to claim later, 'My mother used to make quite a pet of me. I was fondled and kissed and called a pretty boy. But later I used to wish I was strong enough to throttle her. What the devil did she bring me into the world for unless she had plenty of money to give me so that I might enjoy myself in it?'

Certainly, the world into which he was born has rightly been described as, 'the beginning of a Dark Age in which there was a progressive degredation of the standards of life under the blight of growing industrialisation', by the historian Dorothy George in her definitive study, *London Life in the Eighteenth Century* (1930).

Mrs George adds: 'Throughout the century, Londoners lived in a world where violence, disorder and brutal punishment were still part of the normal background of life. Newgate, the gallows, the exploits of felons, figured largely in the press and in the current literature of the day. In spite of the bitter irony of Jonathan Wild and the light satire of the *Beggars' Opera*, both are accurate pictures of the manners of the time, and their more lurid incidents are easily surpassed in the records of the Old Bailey.'

The London of 1756 was certainly unrecognisable from today. The population of the city numbered 670,000, which would rise to over 900,000 by the end of the century. Unlike today, it also consisted of a number of self-contained communities: partly due to the difficulty of getting from one part of the town to the other; partly due to the rigid lines between classes, trades and occupations; and mostly because of the dangerous character of many districts which did not encourage casual visitors. The Spitalfields area where Sweeney Todd was born was just such a district — much of it a slum shielding every kind of squalor and savagery, and home to many criminal dens. In the year 1750, according to the *Commons Journals*, it consisted of 2,400 houses, 1000 of which were not rated 'being inhabited by journeymen weavers and other artificers and labourers who cannot support themselves and their families without credit for small sums'.

The Todds as a family were forever in debt, and always on the verge of the starvation and misery which beset the weaving industry during the second half of the eighteenth century. Spital-fields was then known as the silk-weaving district of London, the leading manufacturers living in places such as Spital Square while their weavers occupied tenement or garret they could find nearby. These men were chiefly employed in making ribbons — which were then very much in fashion — or broad silks for the gentry. Most of the weavers worked in small factories, although a few — the more highly skilled — owned or hired their own looms and sold on the silks they produced to the manufacturers. The recurring problem for both master and man was always the same, though — getting paid, as a report of 1764 reveals:

'Many London manufacturers and especially weavers are sometimes much streightened for money, either to pay their men's wages or to find goods to employ them, especially at the dead time of year, and therefore, being forced to pawn some of their goods for what pawnbrokers are pleased to lend on them, they do not only impoverish themselves, and turn away their men, who, for want of work, do with their families become a burthen to the public. Many manufacturers have of late discharged fifty to a hundred men and put as many more upon half work; and in a little time after the distress has been beyond description . . .'

A specific report on the industry in Spitalfields at this same period goes even further: 'The poverty and distress of some of these people is inconceivable; very generally a family in every room with very little bedding, furniture or clothes. The few rags on their backs comprise the principal part of their property.'

Sweeney Todd's father had experienced years of this kind of uncertain living and, as one of the less skilled weavers, rarely earned more than 12 to 15 shillings per week. Even this sum was often under threat from emigrant Irish workers who would accept less, or women and children who could be employed for even smaller amounts. (A woman like Mrs Todd would probably be hired to wind silk at no more than 3 shillings per week.) Occasionally, Mr Todd would be forced to accept the most menial work of all: winding silk onto bobbins which had to be done at home. Evidence suggests he forced his wife and his

Dangerous and unruly – London at the time Sweeney Todd was born.

infant son into doing this task for him, beating them whenever he became drunk.

Apart from the harshness at home, one of young Sweeney's earliest memories was of the famous Spitalfields Silk Weavers Riots which took place in 1765 when he was just ten years old. The mounting sense of unrest among the local weavers about the growing importation of cheap calico which was undercutting their wages finally exploded into violence. The weavers attacked women and girls on the streets who were wearing calico, throwing acid onto their clothes or tearing the gowns off their backs. Soldiers had to be called in to quell the rioters and, during the ensuing mêlée, five weavers were shot and killed.

The violence both frightened and excited young Sweeney Todd. He vowed there and then that his father's profession was not for him — there had to be a better and easier way of making money.

The boy had, though, already found one place to escape from the drudgery of his daily life — the Tower of London which was less than a mile away from his home. It was an ideal place to go when his parents were either drunkenly brawling or asleep.

There was something about the grim and sombre mass of the Tower and its association with the darker history of England ever since it had been built by William the Conqueror in 1078, that appealed to young Sweeney's increasingly gloomy nature. He had, after all, little to smile about in his life and took a ghoulish sense of pleasure from haunting the edifice on the banks of the River Thames. The awe which the huge building was intended to inspire in the citizens of London certainly had its influence upon him.

Today, of course, the Tower serves primarily as a museum; but in its time it has also been a fortress, royal palace, armoury, mint, and, perhaps most surprisingly of all, until 1835 it was also a royal zoo. It was, though, primarily intended as a prison for political prisoners. Within its massive and forbidding walls, many distinguished men and women were incarcerated including four kings and such famous historical figures as Sir Thomas More, Anne Boleyn, Lady Jane Grey and Archbishop Laud. For many, their stay in the Tower of London ended with a short walk to the scaffold.

The fortress was not only famous for its prisoners, but also its unique collection of instruments of torture which the public was allowed to view in the hope it would discourage them from crime or civil disobedience. Young Todd, we are told, came first to peer at the animals in the zoo and then to linger over the bloodied torture weapons.

The Lion Tower was a favourite spot with many visitors. It housed a number of superb lions as well as several tigers, leopards, black bears and wolves. The warders, however, had none of the finer feelings of the modern zoo attendants — they apparently delighted in poking the creatures with long poles 'to make them lively for visitors,' according to a mid-eighteenth century account. This same source relates that one incautious warden who stuck his arm into the lion's den had a hand bitten off, while a leopard that broke loose 'jumped on the back of a sentinal and half ate him up'.

Excited by watching the lions being fed on huge beef bones of a kind that had never once crossed the Todd's table, Sweeney would then visit the places of torture and feast his eyes on the instruments of madness and death. There was the 'Little Ease', a hole under the White Tower just 18 inches wide, 4 feet high and 2 feet deep into which a prisoner would be forced so that his head was pressed down onto his chest and he could neither sit down or lean. Perhaps even more ghastly were the lower cells which flooded when the tide came in and were also plagued with starving rats. Here prisoners were put for the purpose of extorting confessions: as the water rose, the unfortunate occupants risked death either by drowning or by having the flesh torn from their backs by the sharp teeth of the ravening hoardes of rodents.

In the rooms through which Sweeney Todd roamed were to be seen terrifying thumbscrews; the 'iron gauntlets' which suspended a prisoner from the ceiling by his hands; the fearsome rack that could literally tear a prisoner's joints from his sockets; and the notorious 'Scavenger's Daughter'. This consisted of iron hoops which were tightened around a victim's body by the executioner until blood began to spurt from every orifice and death seemed like a mercy.

Today such sights would probably be considered unsuitable viewing for impressionable young minds, but dozens of urchins from the slums like Sweeney Todd feasted their eyes on these horrors and listened with rapt attention whenever a warden proceeded to give a suitably embellished and invariably gruesome description of their use to visitors.

There was, however, nothing to attract Sweeney — or anyone else for that mater — to the nearby River Thames in the 1760s. An odious mixture of household refuse, plus the waste from factories and open latrines along the banks — all of which poured directly into the Thames — had earned it the reputation of the dirtiest river in Europe. Small wonder that those who ventured near the water, which varied in colour from dark green to black, ran a very real danger of contracting cholera, typhus, smallpox or tuberculosis.

Only during the depth of winter did the Thames hold any sort of attraction for Londoners. For during particularly hard winters, the river froze over and 'Frost Fairs' would be held on the ice when rows of booths would be set up offering food, drink and amusements. Records indicate that there were a number of famous Frost Fairs during the eighteenth century, including one in 1715 — of which there are numerous illustrations — and another in 1739 when frost and strong winds also combined to cause £100,000 damage to shipping in the river and froze a number of people to death on land and at sea.

A more prolonged winter still hit London in 1768 when Sweeney Todd was twelve years old. Although the Thames froze over, few people had any thought of enjoying themselves, so intense was the cold. As one bitterly cold week followed another, coal became increasingly scarce and expensive and few people had the means of maintaining any kind of continual heating. Dozens died in their own homes, and a shoemaker found frozen to death in his stall was just one of several tradespeople who went to work when he should have remained at home.

Among those who did remain at home were the Todd family in Brick Lane. With no work, Sweeney's parents spent their last money on gin and ignored the plaintive cries of their desperate son. Their agony did not continue long, however. For Sweeney awoke one morning as the pale grey light of another bitterly cold day broke into the tenement to find that both his parents had gone. He was never to see either again. Not surprisingly, he nursed a resentment against both for the rest of his life.

Quite what happened to the Todds is unknown: possibly they went searching for more gin and died of cold in the streets. If so, their bodies would have been heaped up with all the others who collapsed in the streets during that terrible winter, and then thrown into a pauper's grave. Certainly, Sweeney Todd never found out what had happened to his parents, although later when arrested for his crimes he invented another typically outrageous lie about his origins and parenthood.

'The church I was christened at was burnt down the day after, and all the books burned,' he told one of his interrogators. 'My father and mother are dead, and the nurse was hanged and the doctor cut his throat.'

There is mystery, too, surrounding the details of how Sweeney himself survived that terrible winter and was next heard of working as an apprentice to a cutler in Holborn. It is reasonable to conject that the resourcefulness and cunning which were later to serve him so well when he began his career of crime came to his aid then, too.

Child labour was a part of every London trade and each tradesman had his apprentice — some even had several. Those children whose parents had been able to give them a basic education could be apprenticed to a tradesman on payment of a fee and might well expect to earn a few pounds a year during their apprenticeship. But what of the others like Sweeney Todd? Historian Dorothy George explains the fate of all such orphans of the streets:

'One of the worst results of the social conditions of this period was the large number of children entirely abandoned to the streets as vagrants or thrown on the tender mercies of the parish. It was the duty of the parish according to the famous Act of 1601 to nurse all of these and to apprentice them when they were old enough.

'Any person, master or journeyman, man or woman, housekeeper or lodger, who would undertake to provide food, lodging and instruction, could take an apprentice. All the earnings of that apprentice, whether they were for the master or a third person, became the property of the master.'

Such a system was obviously open to the most terrible abuses, and Mrs George quotes a report of 1768 which graphically highlights the plight of many youngsters:

'The master may be a tiger in cruelty, he may beat, abuse, strip naked, starve or do what he will to the poor innocent lad, few people take much notice, and the officers who put him out the least of anybody. The greatest part of those who now take poor apprentices are the most indigent and dishonest, and it is the fate of many a poor child, not only to be half-starved and sometimes bred up in no trade, but to be forced to thieve and steal for his master, and so is brought to the gallows into the bargain.'

There is no evidence that Sweeney Todd's master was any better or worse than these men, but he certainly played a part in setting the boy on the road to the gallows.

John Crook was the singularly appropriate name of the man to whom Sweeney Todd was bound. His shop was in Great Turnstile, Holborn. The sign above his window combined a pistol and the letter 'C', which stood for his name.

Cutlers in the eighteenth century were, in fact, dexterous and ingenious artisans who made a whole variety of objects including 'Tinder boxes, Toothpick Cases, Gun Hammers, Wig Springs, Back-Gammon Tables, Saw Strops, Squirrel Chains, Tobacco Tongs, Line Rowls and "Best Battle Gunpowder" ' according to the advertisement of one such London tradesman.

It appears that John Crook was also something of a specialist in razors, for his name is to be found listed with half a dozen other razor makers in London at this time including Edward Tymperon who had premises in Drury Lane and a certain Alexander Jolly to be found at the sign of 'The Unicorn & Case of Knives' in Compton Street, Soho.

Though nothing is actually known about Sweeney Todd's apprenticeship with John Crook, it certainly lasted for at least two years. That he learned a good deal from his master is also fairly evident because of the skill he was later to show in designing and operating the revolving chair in his barber shop. It also seems quite safe to assume that he learned all about razors.

The relationship between the apprentice and his master came to an abrupt end sometime during the year of 1770, however. The boy was accused of petty theft, hauled before a magistrate, and sentenced to five years imprisonment in Newgate Prison. He was just fourteen years old.

Harsh as this sentence seems today, Sweeney Todd was, in

fact, quite lucky to escape with his life. For at this time there were still more than 200 crimes on the statute books that were punishable by hanging — and these included such simple acts as stealing more than a shilling as a pick-pocket or taking goods worth more than 25 pence from a shop.

Whatever Sweeney Todd's crime was, there seems little doubt that he entered prison feeling even more bitter at life. And there that bitterness was to turn first to resentment, and then to a burning desire for revenge.

4

The Cut-throat Killer

Newgate Prison, into which the young Sweeney Todd was unceremoniously bundled in 1770, was a massive and grim fortress which stood on the site occupied today by the Central Criminal Court, the Old Bailey. Indeed, it is an interesting fact that when the notorious gaol was finally pulled down in 1904 some of its stones were used in the building of the present famous London courthouse.

Newgate was, in 1770, one of seven London gates which marked the boundaries of the city: the others were Ludgate, Moorgate, Cripplegate, Bishopsgate, Aldersgate and Aldgate. Temple Bar, which also features in our story, was also a gate erected for ceremonial purposes at the extent of the city liberties.

In company with the city's other western gates — Ludgate and Cripplegate — Newgate served as a prison, though in its case it was primarily for the custody of the common criminals of London and Middlesex. The great grey edifice spanned the roadway of Newgate Street and consisted of two annexes, four storeys high, which were linked by staircases and passageways. The exterior of the building was ornamented with pilasters and statues, one of these being the figure of Liberty with a cat coiled at her feet — and therein lay a story.

From the twelfth century, only the chambers on top of Newgate had served as a gaol, but it had become a prison proper in the fifteenth century thanks to money donated in the will of Sir Richard Whittington — the legendary mayor who walked to London with his cat — who had died in 1423. However, the building suffered badly in the Great Fire of London in 1666 and was almost completely rebuilt. By the late eighteenth century it had become notorious throughout the kingdom.

Apart from the dank and stiffling cells of Newgate which had earned it a terrifying reputation among the law-breaking fraternity, the prison was also notorious with the general public because of the distinguished list of its inmates. This included such master criminals as the pirate, Captain Kidd; James McLean the highwayman; the 'prince of thieves' Jonathan Wild; and the great escaper, Jack Sheppard. Alongside these luminaries were any number of pick-pockets, forgers, burglars and petty thieves of all descriptions. Their ages ranged from mere children of ten to old lags in their seventies. One famous visitor to Newgate, Charles Dickens, was so struck by the young pick-pockets he saw there that he used a group of them as the models for his famous novel, *Oliver Twist*, first published in serial form between 1837 and 1839.

A favourite pastime of certain Londoners was to come and stare at the criminals in Newgate — especially the notorious ones like James McLean and Jack Sheppard. On payment of about three shillings, these visitors were allowed to enter the forbidding walls and stare at the unfortunates in their cells. The more fashionable visitor always made sure they carried a handkerchief soaked in vinegar to counteract the fetid air of the prison and its inmates.

Prior to 1728 many common criminals like Sweeney Todd had been thrown into the Condemned Hold, a mass dungeon on the ground floor that had only a solitary window and was entered by a heavy door topped with spikes which opened onto the entrance hallway of the prison. This had now been replaced by fifteen new cells. Each measured just 9 feet by 7 feet, and was illuminated by a double-grated window. Here the prisoners lived out much of their sentences, although they were allowed out to visit the 'day room' where they could mingle with friends and — if they had any money — receive visitors.

For many years, the gaolers at Newgate had supplemented their meagre wages by extorting money from prisoners. In the main this would 'buy' the men visits from family and relatives,

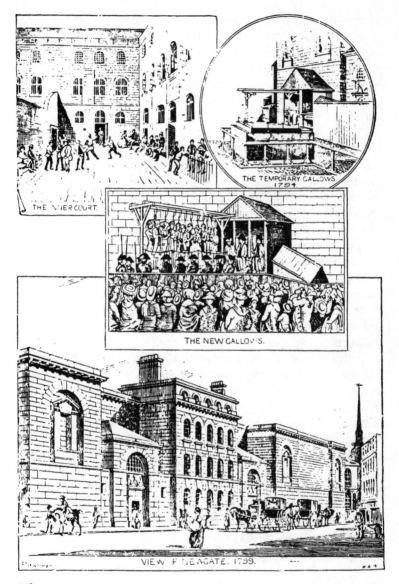

THE TEMPORARY GALLOWS.
1794

THE NEW GALLOWS.

THE INNER COURT.

VIEW OF NEWGATE. 1799.

The notorious Newgate Prison in 1799.

though the more unscrupulous custodians would also threaten to place those who had committed petty crimes in the same cells as violent criminals unless they were paid off. Though this practice was by no means as prevalent when young Todd entered Newgate, those prisoners who had the wherewithal to grease a gaoler's palm certainly enjoyed an easier time of it during their sentence.

Money was, in fact, necessary to even survive in Newgate — for without it a prisoner would soon find himself short of proper clothing to protect himself from the dankness and cold, or without a regular supply of food that was edible. Quickly realising this, the young Sweeney Todd lost no time in looking for an opportunity to keep himself warm and fed. He found it in the shape of a grizzled old barber named Plummer who was serving ten years for embezzlement.

Plummer had apparently swindled money from one of his fashionable London clients, and was then in the fourth year of his imprisonment. He had not wasted the years, though — for there were plenty of the better-off prisoners who liked a shave, and anyone who fell ill had no one but the barber to turn to for treatment.

At this period of time in history, the barber actually played a considerably more extensive role in society than today: he was, in fact, both hairdresser and doctor. People went to him for shaves and haircuts as well as treatment for any minor bodily complaints. Some barbers were even surgeons and quite capable of performing minor operations such as removing a gangrenous arm or leg. Indeed, the ability to wield a blade on human flesh and bones was a prequisite of real success in the trade. (Records indicate that some London barbers even traded in spirits — a useful sideline, no doubt, with customers about to go under the knife who would doubtless be more than willing to pay for a strong tot of brandy or two!)

It is interesting to note that the famous striped pole which has been a feature outside barbers' shops for many years is a remnant from these days. The pole itself represents the staff which the 'barber-surgeon' gave his patient to hold while he was being bled, to encourage the blood to flow. The red, black or blue band painted around the pole represents the ribbon or garter with which the arm of the customer was bound up after the operation.

In a filthy and disease-ridden place like Newgate, the services of the barber Plummer were no doubt much in demand. And Sweeney Todd had the good fortune to enter the prison just as the youngster who had served as the barber's assistant — or 'soap boy' — was being discharged. The new inmate lost no time in boasting to Plummer that he had worked for a cutler and was experienced in sharpening razors and generally looking after the implements of a barber's trade. Whether he told the older man precisely *why* he was now incarcerated we have no way of knowing.

Plummer was evidently impressed enough by the boy to give him the job. He may also have liked Sweeney's touch of cunning, for the barber was still up to his old tricks swindling money from fellow prisoners and gaolers alike. There is no doubt Sweeney Todd learned quickly from his new master — becoming dextrous with the soap brush and deft at lifting small change from the pockets of his master's clients as they reclined in his chair. The boy had, of course, to hand over these ill-gotten gains to Plummer, but was happy to do so in return for the food and clothing and occasional privileges the job earned him. He was, though, always sorry to see the barber's razors carefully collected up by the gaolers at the end of each day — for he would dearly have loved to purloin one for his own use. It seemed obvious to the boy that it was as easy to scrape the whiskers from a man's chin as it would be to slit his throat while he sat, so unaware and vulnerable, in the shaving chair. Clearly, Fate was inexhorably moving Sweeney Todd closer towards his destiny.

Those prisoners about to be executed were always allowed a special shave before they were hung and Todd invariably accompanied Plummer on these assignments. It was the one place that conversation was permitted, too; for in the main part of Newgate a rule of silence was rigidly enforced and those who broke it were flogged. And as the condemned man had probably recently received visitors, it was another way of finding out what was happening in the world beyond the walls of Newgate.

The public outside were evidently just as interested in what was going on *inside* Newgate, for a year after Sweeney Todd had entered the prison, the first issue of a weekly, penny publication, *The Newgate Calendar; or, Malefactor's Bloody Register*, was issued by an astute London publisher named J. Cooke. This famous record of crimes and trials was undoubtedly a forerunner of the most sensational of today's tabloid newspapers. Its aim — according to a banner on the front page — was to feature 'Genuine and Circumstantial Narratives of the Lives and Transactions, Various Exploits and Dying Speeches, of the Most Notorious Criminals of Both Sexes.'

The publication, printed in double columns of miniscule type on eight pages of flimsy paper, featured a single lurid illustration on the front cover, and inside all the most gruesome and dramatic tales of forgery, robbery and murder the editor could unearth. The earliest cases were from 1700 and virtually every one ended in a hanging.

The success of *The Newgate Calendar* was to inspire several imitators, as well as generating an interest in true crime that has continued to flourish and develop to the present day. As historian Rayner Heppenstall wrote in his *Reflections on the Newgate Calendar* (1975):

'*The Newgate Calendar* itself is literature, for the most part of a rather poor kind, fit only to inspire literature in others. The best of it is evidence heard in court, which, once transcribed and published, is literature. Law itself is literature. In court, lawyers compose literature with great deliberation. The spontaneous cut-and-thrust of courtroom drama on stage, screen or radio is rarely heard in court. There, judges and counsel dictate their works slowly to the clerk of the court and to reporters, much as Henry James dictated his to a devoted secretary or as modern authors may dictate theirs to tape recorders, with all the more care because it will not be possible for them to make alterations in the transcript.'

Mr Heppenstall also adds, 'The later Calendars were among

the first products of a reforming age which looked back fascinated at one during which too many were hanged for too little.'

The Newgate Calendar was to run in one form or another
until 1825, in all covering over a thousand cases from the years
1701 to 1825. An enterprising publisher named E. Harrison who
operated in Salisbury Square, Fleet Street, revived the idea in
1864 as *The New Newgate Calendar*, expanding the format to
sixteen pages, but mingling fiction amongst the factual accounts
of crimes, many of which had been lifted, almost untouched,
from the pages of its predecessor.

It is doubtful whether Sweeney Todd knew anything about
The Newgate Calendar when it was launched — or would even
have tried to read it if he did, for there is evidence that he
was no more than semi-literate at the time of his arrest. He was,
though, to feature in its pages when justice finally caught up
with him, as we shall discover later.

Despite his association with the barber Plummer, Todd did
not escape the vindictiveness of some of the Newgate gaolers or
the cruelty of a number of his fellow inmates. His privileged
position caused resentment among some of the other youthful
offenders and he took several cruel beatings during his five year
imprisonment. One convicted murderer apparently beat him to
within an inch of his life when he caught the boy pilfering
through his few possessions. Plummer is said to have stood by
while this punishment was meted out — probably from a mixture
of fear and cowardice — though he would undoubtedly have
benefited from any of his soap boy's plunder.

The resentment that Sweeney Todd nursed against society
certainly built up as the five years of his prison sentence dragged
by; although he did not allow this to deter him from learning
all about his master's profession. He already knew it would be
the trade he would follow once he was released from
Newgate...

The Sweeney Todd who at last walked free from Newgate
Prison in the autumn of 1775 was now a strapping nineteen-
year-old with a profession. But the years had also made him a
morose, bitter and cruel man. Although it is doubtful whether

he actually planned a life of crime — he had, after all, just sacrificed five years because of it — his ambition was to make money, and he had few scruples about how he was going to do this.

Sweeney's immediate need, though, was to earn his daily bread and in order to do this he joined the ranks of London's 'Flying Barbers'. These men, who were commonplace in eighteenth-century England, travelled wherever there was the likelihood of custom, setting themselves up on street corners, in markets or at fairs, and offering their services to passersby. It was a tough business where men would fight over a favourite pitch, and Sweeney Todd undoubtedly had to bloody more than a few other 'Flying Barbers' in order to survive and make his way.

But survive he did. Five years after his release from Newgate Prison, the young barber had apparently earned enough to be operating from his own premises near Hyde Park Corner. There he prospered, until one night just before Christmas 1784.

There is evidence that Todd was being helped in his business by a young woman, though what their relationship was remains a mystery. Certainly, there is no record of the barber ever marrying, though it is possible that he may have referred to her as his wife for the benefit of his more refined clientele. What we *do* know is that Sweeney Todd's temper was already getting the better of him when he became annoyed, and this unfortunate woman probably bore the brunt of his rages whenever they occurred.

The events which were to dramatically change the course of Sweeney Todd's life and lead him to the London street with which his name is now associated, occurred on 1 December 1784. They are related in a single paragraph which appeared in *The Annual Register* under the heading, 'A Barbarous Barber':

'A most remarkable murder was perpetrated in the following manner by a journeyman barber that lived near Hyde Park Corner, who had been jealous of his wife, but could in no way bring this home to her. A young gentleman, by chance coming into the barber's shop to be shaved and dressed, and being in *liquor, mentioned having seen a fine girl in Hamilton Street, from whom he had had certain favours the night before, and at the same time describing her person. The barber, concluding this to be his wife, and in the height of his frenzy, cut the young gentleman's throat from ear to ear and absconded.'*

The details are certainly sparse, and though the disappearing barber is not mentioned by name — as few criminals were in the press of the time until brought to trial — the events matched the known facts about Sweeney Todd's whereabouts in the last days of 1784.

Although a hue and cry was raised shortly after the discovery of the murder by the next customer who entered the barber's shop and found the blood-soaked corpse slumped in the shaving chair, no sign of the man who had shaved him was ever reported again in Hyde Park Corner. 'Mrs Todd' appears to have been none too disturbed by the disappearance, however, and rumour has it that by the New Year she was already living with another tradesman in the district.

It has to be admitted that the evidence Sweeney Todd committed this crime remains circumstantial at best. Indeed, the grounds are primarily a confession by the man himself after he was finally arrested for his serial killings.

'My first 'un was a young gent at Hyde Park Corner,' he is reported as saying. 'Slit him from ear to ear, I did.'

There is, however, no disputing the facts about where he next came to light and set up in business — Fleet Street. Nor that in the cramped and dingy front room of a little shop there, he would combine the ingenuity of a cutler with the skill of a barber to begin an era of murder and bloodshed that is unique in the annals of crime.

5

The Curious World of Fleet Street

No one knows why Sweeney Todd decided to set up his barber's pole outside a little shop at the higher end of Fleet Street, right in the shadow of Temple Bar, in the year 1785.

At first sight it seemed a curious choice for a man who had spent five years of his life imprisoned in another of London's city gates. But prices were undoubtedly cheaper there than in Covent Garden or Drury Lane — two of the most popular localities for the city's barbers — and it is quite feasible that the astute Todd realised his chances of success were better with fewer rivals on his doorstep. Or perhaps — just perhaps — he was already hatching his nefarious plans and wanted to distance himself from the centre of his profession. Maybe he even had some knowledge of the labyrinth of passageways beneath the street which would prove to be of great value in sustaining his terrible reign of crime for over a decade. All we can do from this distance in time is to conject...

The Fleet Street of the last quarter of the eighteenth century was, of course, very different from that of today. Just a few years ago it was known around the world as the 'Street of Ink', the home for some of the most important and influential newspapers in Europe including the *Daily Express*, the *Daily Telegraph*, the *Observer*, the *Daily Mail*, the *Sun* and the *News of the World*. But industrial disputes and the arrival of computer technology has seen them all depart and now only the memory remains. Fleet Street is, though, still a place worth visiting, if only to try and imagine just what it must have been like when Sweeney Todd lived there. Where today there are only orderly office buildings and commercial premises, there was then a huddle of squalid and disreputable shops, taverns and mean dwellings of all shapes and sizes. Yet the history of the place proves to be as fascinating and bizarre as any to be found within the confines of the metropolis.

Fleet Street is often wrongly associated in people's mind with the old Fleet Prison which actually stood some distance away on the eastern side of what is now Farringdon Street. It did, though, get its name from the infamous Fleet Ditch which now-adays runs in a sewer beneath Bridge Street, and was crossed by the Fleet Bridge (a site now occupied by Ludgate Circus).

For centuries the Ditch was used by the local residents as a dumping place for all their household rubbish and offal; and not surprisingly it earned an unenviable reputation for its stomach-turning appearance and appalling stench. Indeed, records indicate that the Ditch retained its filthy and insanitary state well into the eighteenth century.

The street itself had been in existence since the days of the Roman occupation of Britain, when it was a road running through open countryside crossing what was then a pleasant little stream. The walls of the Roman city of Augusta — as London was then called — ended where Ludgate Circus now stands, and a Pratorian camp was permanently located in the district. The Romans also selected the area as a burial spot for soldiers and over the years human remains of one sort and another have been found during the course of building work and excavations in Fleet Street.

Perhaps the importance that the Romans placed on the area lead to its gradual development into a fashionable district, for certainly by 1325 it was notable enough to be referred to in one history as 'Fletestrete in the suburb of London'. By 1543, records show it was quite extensively developed with a number of important houses, several churches and a landmark known as The Temple.

Today, the location of that Temple, which has given its name to the area at the top of Fleet Street which separates if from The Strand — the Temple Bar is marked by a memorial statue known as The Griffin, which divides the traffic near the junction with Chancery Lane. Prior to the erection of this striking sculpture of the winged creature from mythology, there had been, since at least the twelfth century, a demarkation line on the spot to mark the western boundary of the city of London. The very earliest 'bar' was no more than a chain hung between two posts and was probably erected by the Templars to indicate the extent of their lands at that time.

Later, actual gates were constructed across the road, and in the reign of James I a proper archway was built. In 1672 this was replaced by a new Temple Bar of Portland Stone designed by Sir Christopher Wren which remained on the site until 1878. Then, due to the enormous increase in London's traffic which had made the spot terribly congested, it was decided to remove the archway. It was thereupon summarily sold to a London brewer who had it removed to the grounds of his home at Theobald's Park in Hertfordshire where it has remained to this day.

Though there can be no denying that the Temple Bar was a striking-looking construction and many Londoners were sorry to see it go, it had earned a rather sinister reputation which made it a place to avoid by night. For years, it was customary for the heads of executed criminals to be placed on iron spikes and stuck up on the top of the gateway. The English diarist and novelist, John Evelyn, who frequently had to pass this way called the Temple 'a dismal sight' and the array of traitors' heads upon it 'a revolting spectacle'.

Three heads which had been on the Temple since 1746 were still there when Sweeney Todd took up his residence just a stone's throw away. A curious contemporary print of these macabre relics and a description of two of the men who had lost their heads still exists. The picture (reproduced here) is all the more curious because of the devil figure looking down in triumph and waving a banner on which are inscribed the words, 'A Crown or a Grave'. Underneath the print were the following verses:

Observe the banner which would enslave,
Which ruined traitors did so proudly wave.
The devil seems the project to despise;
A fiend confused from off the trophy flies.

A gruesome eighteenth-century print of decapitated heads at Temple Bar.

While trembling rebels at the fabric gaze,
And dread their fate with horror and amaze,
Let Briton's sons the emblematic view,
And plainly see what to rebellion's due.

Sweeney Todd would in all probability have known the history of two of the heads on the iron poles, those of Townley and Fletcher; but for the benefit of the reader let me quote this brief history from Walter Thornbury's excellent book, *Haunted London* (1880), which also reprinted the gruesome illustration:

'The heads of Fletcher and Townley were put up on Temple Bar on August 2, 1746. On August 16, Horace Walpole wrote to his friend Montague to say that he had "passed under the new heads at Temple Bar, where people made a trade of letting spy-glasses at a halfpenny a look".

'Townley was a young officer about 38 years of age, born at Wigan, and of a good family. He had been 15 years abroad in the French army, and was close to the Duke of Berwick when the duke's head was shot off at the seige of Philipsburgh. When the Highlanders came into England he met them near Preston, and received from the young Pretender a commission to raise a regiment of foot soldiers. He had been also commandant at Carlisle and directed the sallies from thence before his capture and trial.

'Fletcher, a young linen chapman at Salford, had been seen pulling off his hat and shouting when a sergeant and a drummer were beating up for volunteers at the Manchester Exchange. He had been seen also at Carlisle, dressed as an officer, with a white cockade in his hat and a plaid sash round his waist.

'Who the other Jacobite shown upon the Temple roof and most likely executed for treason with these two I have no idea.'

Perhaps not surprisingly, the heads often attracted the wrong kind of attention from people who went further than merely staring at them. In January 1766, for instance, a man was arrested for 'discharging musket-balls from a steel cross-bow' at the heads because he believed 'it was not sufficient that traitors should merely suffer death', Walter Thornbury tells us. While in April

1772 'one of the rebel heads fell down after a storm' and was quickly hurried away and sold as a relic in a nearby public house.

According to other sources, there were people still living in Fleet Street at the end of the nineteenth century who could remember seeing the decomposing heads hanging on the Temple Bar until they finally fell off into the street below. Indeed, the last of the iron spikes was not actually removed from the arch until the middle of the 1800s.

Fleet Street itself had been swallowed up in the sprawl of London by the sixteenth century, and its character and that of its residents had also changed rapidly. To be sure, there were still a number of fine buildings facing the street; but behind them where there had once been fields and gardens things were very different indeed. The area had, in fact, become one of lawlessness and debauchery, as this report from the year 1570 graphically illustrates:

'The poor watchmen of the parish of St Bride's, Fleet Street, being called forth on Thursday night (April 1570) to aid the sheriff in quieting a broil in Fleet Street, were all wounded, and are likely to be cripples for ever.'

In his definitive study of the area, *Annals of Fleet Street* (1912), E. Beresford Chancellor explains the reason for this change of character:

'The presence in the street of a large number of taverns had much to do with this state of affairs,' he wrote, 'and the defective means of policing the streets made it an easy matter for the lawless to perpetrate their daring deeds, and then to hurry off to the safe asylum of the contiguous byways and alleys, or to seek shelter in the wilds of Whitefriars.'

Mr Chancellor goes on to say that the Domestic State Papers are full of accounts of murders, robberies and thefts in Fleet Street during the times of the Tudors and their successors. Drawing a parallel with his own times, the author added, 'You might not incur the risk of being run down by a motor bus or taxicab, but you stood a very good chance of being dirked or clubbed if you were dissipated enough to be out of doors after, say, nine o'clock in the evening.'

But for those criminals who were caught, Mr Chancellor says, retribution was swift — for it was not unusual for a person to be promptly hung near the very scene of their crime. The sight of a gibbet newly erected bearing its latest grisly victim was not at all an unusual one to the people of Fleet Street. Indeed, a famous instance was still a popular topic of conversation when Sweeney Todd moved into the area.

The case, which happened in 1728, was all the more intriguing because the killer was a twenty-five-year-old woman, Sarah Malcolm, who had killed her mistress and two fellow servants. She had cut the throat of one of her victims and strangled the other two. What made Sarah notorious was the fact that many people believed she was innocent and regarded her as something of a heroine. The famous painter Hogarth, in fact, visited the young woman in her cell and painted her portrait.

Whatever the public might have thought, nothing could save Sarah Malcolm from the gallows, and it was decreed that she should suffer her punishment at the scene of her crimes. To this end, she was hanged in Fleet Street at a point just between Mitre Court and Fetter Lane. Thousands crammed the area to see her last moments as she climbed onto the gallows, 'her cheeks painted in honour of the occasion' according to one contemporary account.

Significantly, Sarah's fame in the annals of crime might well be better known today but for the arrival in the vicinity just a short while later of Sweeney Todd . . .

The evil and insanitary dens behind the facade of Fleet Street were, hardly surprisingly, prime targets for both fire and plague. Records indicate that in the year 1625 alone, over 500 people in the parish died from cholera. The west side of Fleet Street — perhaps the poorest of all the districts — was also devastated by the Great Fire of London in 1666. Samuel Pepys noted in his *Diary* that he had seen the flames 'running downe to Fleet Street'. Although systematic rebuilding in 1677 made some difference to the neighbourhood — and by widening the thoroughfare the conditions were made generally less insanitary — there was still no shifting the criminal fraternity who were too firmly entrenched in their hideouts to be displaced by either disease or flames.

Despite these unruly elements, Fleet Street was nevertheless acting as a magnet to many Londoners, and by the eighteenth century some of its taverns were a favourite meeting place for the exchange of gossip and news. Indeed, it was in these places that the first 'news sheets' were written and the plans laid for London's first daily papers.

The great forerunner of the newspaper industry was the *Daily Courant* which appeared in 1702 published 'for E. Mallet against the Ditch at Fleet Bridge'. Within a few years it was to have several rivals all of whom would cluster nearby in Fleet Street. Several booksellers and publishers likewise chose to locate themselves here — including the notorious Edmund Curll who issued a string of pornographic works from his ostensibly inoffensive address, 'at the sign of the Dial & Bible, against St Dunstan's Church'.

It is perhaps just worth noting that today's visitor to Fleet Street seeking an example of the kind of atmosphere which nurtured this creativity can do no better than to visit the famous 'Cheshire Cheese' in Wine Court which, with its low-beamed rooms and sawdust-strewn wooden floors, is still redolent with the ghosts of its famous regulars like Dr Johnson, Addison, Boswell, Dickens, and many more.

A quite different sort of attraction for the ordinary men and women were the exhibitions and shows staged on Fleet Street, as E. Beresford Chancellor has also explained:

'The Eighteenth Century was the heyday of "shows" for which the thoroughfare became noted. The exhibition of monsters, contortionists, fire-eaters, waxworks and moving pictures were more to the taste of Fleet Street patrons than the concord of sweet sounds, or music married to immortal verse. Ben Jonson (in *Every Man in his Humour*) refers to "a new motion of the City of Nineveh, with Jonas and the whale" being exhibited at Fleet Bridge; and when he makes Knowell end a speech with the words, "Here within this place is to be seen the true, rare and accomplished monster, a miracle of nature," he is probably copying some such announcement seen by him in front of one of the Fleet Street shows.

'Nothing seemed then to come amiss to the curiosity of the public. It was as happy in looking at the giants striking the hours on St Dunstan's clock as in inspecting a model of Amsterdam "thirty feet long" or in regaling its sight on a legless child, measuring but eighteen inches, who was to be seen at a grocer's in Shoe Lane at the sign of the "Eagles and Child". All kinds of wonderful and fearsome animals attracted crowds, from a great Lincolnshire ox, nineteen hands high, to an old she-dromedary and her young one.'

'The Duke of Marlborough's Head at Shoe Lane seems to have been a great centre of attraction,' Mr Chancellor adds, 'for here, at various times, were exhibited a "moving picture"; "The Great Posture-Master of Europe" who "extends his body into all deformed shapes"; and a certain De Hightrehight who, besides eating burning coals, satisfied a curious appetite by sucking a red-hot poker five times a day. Automaton clocks and giants and dwarfs proved great "draws" — indeed Fleet Street was quite noted for the latter.'

Perhaps, however, the greatest of all the attractions in Fleet Street at this time was Mrs Salmon's Waxworks which drew thousands of curiosity seekers for over half a century. These figures had actually all been made somewhat earlier by the remarkable Mrs Salmon and exhibited in Aldersgate until her death in 1760 at the ripe old age of ninety. Thereafter they were purchased by a man named Clark who moved them into new premises at 189 Fleet Street, where they remained a constant source of amazement until 1812 when the whole collection was inexplicably broken up and sold.

It is an interesting thought that this show was almost next door to Sweeney Todd's new premises and many customers must have passed the one on their way to the other. Though an hour or so of wonder and amusement awaited the clients of Mrs

Salmon's Waxworks, an unpleasant death was to be the fate of many of those who chose to enter the barber's premises.

Interestingly, too, 189 Fleet Street was later taken over by a man named Carter who ran another successful business there for close on seventy years. His profession? A hairdresser.

This, then, was the spot in which Sweeney Todd decided to open his business in 1785. A little corner of London famous for its lawlessness and taste for the macabre. It was, in truth, ideally suited for a man who had a taste for both and was soon to combine them with deadly efficiency.

6

Easy Shaving for a Penny

Historians have had a lot of harmless fun over the years arguing about the exact address of Sweeney Todd's shop in Fleet Street. The debate has taken on something of the fascination of the search for 221B Baker Street, the famous address of London's greatest detective, Sherlock Holmes. The difference is that we *know* the Great Detective was fiction and his creator, Sir Arthur Conan Doyle, merely picked the address now occupied by the Abbey National Building Society because it was suitable for his purpose.

The various localities for the site where Todd hung out his sign, 'Easy shaving for a penny — As good as you will find any,' are, however, worth considering in connection with what occurred later during the barber's relationship with his partner-in-crime, Mrs Lovett.

In one of the earliest fictionalisations of Todd's life, *Sweeney Todd, The Demon Barber of Fleet Street*, written anonymously for the London publishing firm of Charles Fox in 1878, his address is given as 69 Fleet Fleet.

'If you have any wish to take a greater criminal than I,' Mrs Lovett told the Bow Street Runners upon her arrest, 'then go to the shop of one Sweeney Todd, a barber, in Fleet Street. His number is sixty-nine. Seize him and I shall be content.'

The choice of this number by the writer is curious and obviously inaccurate — for the address is actually towards the lower end of Fleet Street near Ludgate Circus, and contradicts all the known facts about which side of the street the shop was situated on by being on the opposite side of the road.

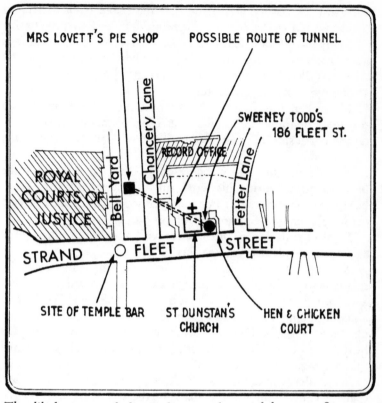

The likely route of the underground tunnel between Sweeney Todd's cellars and Mrs Lovett's pie shop.

Nor is the evidence any better for another possible location, number 154 Fleet Street. This second number was cited in at least two letters about Sweeney Todd published in the scholarly magazine, *Notes & Queries*, during a debate concerning the Demon Barber in the 1890s. When no reader could confirm or deny the claim, interest in the subject faded — and did not reappear until half a century later in 1947.

Then the matter came to public attention again as a result of some demolition work in Fleet Street during which a most surprising discovery was made. Let me quote from the report that appeared in the *London Evening News* of 24 April, 1947.

'Many people are loath to believe that Sweeney Todd was never more substantial than a legend. They are joined today by Alfred Waller, a burly builder's manager, who, hitherto, had no strong opinions on the matter.

'Mr Waller, who is at work on a building in Fleet Street, told me today he thinks he has discovered proof that number 154 — on the north side, opposite Bouverie Street — was the celebrated barber's shop.

The old number 154 is being demolished to make way for new premises. During his work on this enterprise, Mr Waller has found a fanlight and some pieces of wood which were buried below plaster, all bearing the Demon Barber's name.

'Signs of trap-doors, and a cellar with a manhole which leads to a sewer, lend substance to this belief.'

Much as many people must have hoped the claim could be substantiated, the explanation for the signs proved to be disappointingly prosaic. In fact, just prior to the Second World War an enterprising barber had occupied 154 and decided to cash-in on the fame of the Demon Barber of Fleet Street by calling his business 'Sweeney Todd, Barber'. It was, sadly, his old sign board that Mr Waller had uncovered!

The evidence in favour of 186 Fleet Street, beside St Dunstan's Church and standing in the shade of the site of the old Temple Bar, is overwhelming. Not least because of its position in direct line to Bell Yard on the other side of the church where the pie shop was placed, but even more so because of the many passageways and tunnels which had been discovered, providing a link between the two points.

The facts also concur with the description given in the first novelisation of the legend in *The String of Pearls* by Thomas Peckett Prest which appeared in *The People's Periodical* of 21 November, 1846, and to which we shall be returning later for a fuller discussion. The opening paragraph of the story reads:

'Before Fleet Street had reached its present importance, and when George the Third was young, and the figures who used to strike the chimes at old St Dunstan's Church were in all their glory — providing a great impediment to errand-boys on their rounds and a matter of gaping curiosity to country people — there stood close to the sacred edifice a small barber's shop which was kept by a man of the name of Sweeney Todd.'

There is factual evidence to back this piece of fiction, too. The evidence has been brought to light by the historian and researcher W. O. G. Lofts who has greatly assisted me in the research for this book. According to Mr Lofts, during the 1880s, some very old buildings in Fleet Street close to St Dunstan's Church were pulled down. Underneath the cellars of number 186 a large pit of bones was found. 'At first these seemed undeniably like the remains of some of Sweeney Todd's victims,' Mr Lofts says, 'but on closer investigation another possibility became apparent. The old St Dunstan's Church which had been rebuilt about 1830 used to stand east to west and so therefore the bones under 186 could equally have been from the old church vaults.' Indeed they could. But, as we shall see later, they could just as easily have been the bones of some of Todd's victims hidden among older relics to cover up the full enormity of his crimes.

St Dunstan's Church, which was to play such a significant part in the legend of Sweeney Todd, was one of the focal points of Fleet Street in 1785 — as it remains to this day. Although a church has stood on the site since the thirteenth century, the present building only dates from 1833. It is the previous edifice in which we are interested. This building projected further into the thoroughfare than the existing structure — a result of the Great Fire when the surrounding buildings were moved to their previous line in order to give pedestrians and traffic more room.

The earlier St Dunstan's had a tower and a battlemented pediment over the lower windows, but undoubtedly its most striking feature was a clock projecting over the street with two figures which emerged from an alcove to strike each hour. Installed on the church in 1671, the clock became one of the sights of London, not to mention Fleet Street. The two life-like figures represented savages and were known as the 'Giants of St Dunstan's'. They were carved in wood and each was armed with a club with which they struck each quarter of an hour on two bells suspended between them. As the figures swung these clubs, their heads also moved from side to side.

Apart from the many sightseers that the clock attracted to St Dunstan's, it was also considered a fashionable church, and records indicate it was much used by the London gentry for weddings, christenings and burials. None of this, though, prevented the clergy from being constantly worried about the disorderly neighbourhood in which they were situated.

'All around,' one incumbent wrote in the eighteenth century, 'there are shops which cling barnacle-like to the south side and east front harbouring all sorts and descriptions of trades. There are many premises in the vicinity used by lawbreakers and passages running underground beneath them through which the thieves escape after ill-using their victims.'

A maze of small courts and alleyways in the vicinity also made it easy for the pick-pockets and petty crooks to disappear quickly with their spoils, as E. Beresford Chancellor has also written:

'The chief characteristic of the north side of Fleet Street is the number of small courts and alleys which, at that time, were found there. Some have disappeared, like the famous Johnson's Court, which was absorbed in Aderton's Hotel. Some were but means of access to larger areas behind the houses in the main thoroughfare, and have become obliterated in the course of building developments. Not a few, however, still remain, and it is in these exiguous outlets that one can, here and there, best gain an approximate idea of what Fleet Street must have looked like to our fore-fathers.'

But, Mr Chancellor adds succinctly, 'In the days of George the Third, the area was, quite simply, a hot-bed of lawlessness which the authorities stood little chance of penetrating and rarely attempted to.'

According to one report, Sweeney Todd paid £125 for the lease of 186 Fleet Street. His agreement was to pay an annual rental to the Skinners Company of £17.10s per annum and 'consenting to keep the premises in ordinary repair'. Prior to his occupation, the shop had been used by a hosier, but Sweeney converted the ground floor for use as a barber's and kept the upper floors for living accommodation. On one side of the house was a passage known as Hen & Chicken Court which lead into a labyrinth of passageways; while on the other a house occupied by a shoemaker named Whittle.

When Sweeney Todd opened for business it was evident he had not spent a great deal of time or money on preparing the premises. A description written at the turn of the century pictures a building that had probably changed very little in the intervening years.

'The evil-looking house looked as if it had been left there in the days of the dark ages, and had missed the advancing hand of civilization. Its blackened front, its windows shrouded with dirt and rubbish, and its beetling gables impressed those who saw it with feelings of foreboding.'

Todd had, though, advertised his dual role of barber and surgeon with a number of items on display at the shop. A long white pole striped with red projected from the front of the building, and over the door were painted in fat, yellow letters the words 'Sweeney Todd, Barber'. Behind the front windows, Todd arranged several wigs and perukes on blocks roughly shaped like heads. Beside these stood a number of jars filled with what was evidently coagulated blood and some bottles of rotten teeth. These were to advertise his skills at pulling teeth and bleeding clients for minor ailments. A solitary razor, open, hung in one panel of the window below a board proclaiming in rhyming doggrel, 'Easy shaving for a penny – As good as you will find any.'

Inside, the shop was no more impressive. Heavy beams seemed to bring the ceiling down, while the darkened walls only enhanced the general gloom of the place. Two oil lamps hanging on opposite sides of the room were normally only lit as evening began to fall. Underneath one of these on a peg hung a number of dirty-looking sheets, some spotted with blood, which the barber would place around the necks of his customers. A scarred and grimy bench ran the length of the back wall. On this Todd had arranged the tools of his trade including combs, brushes, shaving bowls, some hanks of hair and a number of sharp knives and pincers. Above these, neatly hanging in rows, were a collection of razors, including three Magnum Bonums, the sharpest and most highly regarded of all razors. On the left-hand wall a small fireplace burned lumps of coal to boil the water for shaving and the minor operations, while alongside hung a leather strap on which the barber stropped his razors before attending to each customer. Alternately, he had a stone with which to grind the heavier blades.

The observant visitor might have noticed that the bare wooden floor of the shop bore a number of dark stains, especially around a large, old-fashioned chair standing in the middle of the room. This was made of carved oak and had ornate legs and a high back. But only the very keen-eyed would every have noticed how tightly it was screwed to the floor and the very tiny gaps forming a square around the legs. And by then it might well have been too late . . .

The barber himself was, if anything, even less attractive than his shop. Accounts describe him as a sullen looking figure, with heavy eyebrows, a hard mouth and generally pugnacious features.

'Sweeney Todd was a barber in a small way of business,' says an account published in the *Gentleman's Magazine* of 1853. 'He was always grumbling about how hard times were, dressed in the plainest of clothes and had all the appearance of being a poor man. But there was also something very sinister about him with his pale face and reddish hair. At times he was like some hobgoblin, his strange, dark eyes agleam with greed and cunning.'

Another account in the *Courier* was even less complementary, if a little fanciful: 'Sweeney Todd was a man of middle age, and so repulsive in appearance that it is a wonder that such stray customers who ventured into his shop did not immediately flee from it when the demon in human frame commenced operations. The glitter in his eyes was as keen as the razor he flashed and wielded with the dexterity of one skilled in his craft.

'He was a long, loose-joined, ill-shaped fellow, with a huge mouth filled with black teeth. His hands were of abnormal size, he had immense feet and wiry hair, sometimes bristling with the combs used in his trade. Sweeney Todd also squinted, and was as ugly a wretch as could be seen in a day's march. But people did not pay much attention to him, and let him go his own way, for he seemed a harmless, reserved man, aware of his looks, and consequently avoided the society of his fellow creatures.'

In the shop, the barber invariably wore an apron, keeping a pair of scissors in the pocket. Later it transpired that he also concealed a razor up his sleeve, 'a little habit of mine,' he once said, 'for living in a dangerous place like London.'

When Sweeney did venture out, it was usually on business to visit the houses of wealthier clients whom he would shave or attend to their perukes and wigs. For pleasure, he apparently visited the Bald-faced Stag, 'an evil-looking public house' in Fleur-de-Lis Court off Fetter Lane. Here he would only drink brandy — the memories of what gin had done to his parents haunted him all his life.

Sweeney Todd was clearly a man who kept himself very much to himself in the early period of his career in Fleet Street. Little was known about his habits or who he consorted with, although as time passed he began to be looked upon a little suspiciously, as the *Gentleman's Magazine* also makes clear:

'It was true that all sorts of unpleasant rumours and surmises began to be whispered regarding him, up and down the street; for several people — seafaring men — who had been last known to visit his shop had disappeared as completely as though the earth had opened and swallowed them — but no one could prove that he had anything to do with these disappearances.'

Indeed, this state of affairs was to continue for some years. But behind the shutters of 186 Fleet Street, the man who gave 'Easy shaving for a penny', was actually operating a most diabolical scheme of robbery and murder.

7

The Human Ghoul

The London of 1785 was an almost perfect environment in which a cold and calculating murderer might hope to profit from killing *and* escape detection into the bargain. Human life was held cheap, and for the majority of those dwelling in the city their lives were short, brutish and miserable in the extreme.

Drink was both the comfort and the cause of much of the unhappiness. Hogarth's famous painting of 'Gin Lane' with rows of drunken bodies lying in the streets, customers squabbling in the shops selling spirits, and a general air of decay, squalor, poverty, illness and debauchery accurately sums up the existence of the ordinary men, women and children at this time.

Crime and punishment went virtually unchecked, too. Just the year before, no less a person than the Prime Minister, Lord North, had been held up and robbed by a highwayman in Gunnersbury Lane. These 'knights of the road', who were as popular with the public then as film and rock stars are today, lead a dangerous and colourful life and were expected to thumb their noses at the law and meet their death on the gallows with a smile and a wave to the massed crowds. Despite the fact that over 250 highwaymen were caught and hung in the quarter of a century from 1750, their numbers, if anything, increased.

Punishment was meted out by the authorities with little rhyme or reason. In 1785 alone a total of ninety-seven people were executed, predominantly for minor offences, including a boy of nine accused of breaking a window and a father of eight children who was hanged for stealing a loaf of bread. Small wonder that amidst all the disturbances, immorality and crime on the streets of the city, Samuel Johnson could describe it as, 'London — the needy villain's general home!'

The fact that London was then at a peak of both crime and punishment makes it easier to understand how the odds were stacked in favour of the clever criminal avoiding arrest. Tongues might wag, accusing fingers might point, but justice was still blind in trapping those who were skilled at law-breaking. And this skill might consist of little more than an ability to run quickly or lie convincingly.

Fog, too, was a great assistance to the criminal fraternity. The city had been prone to fogs ever since the first coal fires had been lit there in medieval times — assisted by the fact that London lay beside a river. The whole metropolis and its people were helpless in the grip of these annual fogs and could do nothing to prevent or mitigate them. Sometimes they lasted for months, and it was not unusual for the city to be swathed in cloying billows of greyish-white smoke from November to March. John Evelyn paints a vivid picture of such a scene in one of his *Diary* entries:

'The horrid smoke obscures our churches and makes our palaces look old. It fouls our clothes and corrupts the waters, so that the very rain and refreshing dews that fall in the several seasons precipitate this impure vapour, which with its black and tenacious quality, spots and contaminates whatever is exposed to it.'

These terrifying blankets of fog in which it was barely possible to see a hand in front of your face, were ideal for the perpetration of murder and robbery, allowing the criminal to vanish as quickly as he had arrived. Many people were lost in fogs never to be seen again: some were clubbed down in the streets, others drowned in the murky waters of the Thames, still more swallowed up in the open sewers or the footings of new buildings. Hundreds died from the effects, either directly or indirectly: it was impossible to establish which.

Records show that these fogs were at their worst in the middle of the eighteenth century, one of the thickest on record occurring in 1772 while Sweeney Todd was serving his sentence in

Newgate. Even behind bars, he was no doubt aware of the nightmare of fear, inconvenience and disaster that the fog caused to everyone living in the city.

Looking back on all these factors it is, indeed, easy to understand how, in the London of 1785, Sweeney Todd was able to begin and then carry on for so long and with such impunity his campaign of mass murder.

The barber did not work all alone in his shop in Fleet Street. Like all tradesmen, he employed an apprentice — and in his case several; all of who came into and went from his service with suspicious frequency. The actual number of 'soap boys' employed by Todd is unknown, but it must certainly have approached double figures.

As an employer, Todd treated his apprentices with the same mixture of cruelty and indifference that he himself had received. He was able to recruit 'soap boys' with ease from among the starving vagrants of the capital, or alternately those children from rural hovels whose parents had pushed them off to the city in the hope that it might offer a better means of sustenance. As the historian Dorothy George has explained:

'Thus many children were apprenticed simply as drudges — girls to the lowest conceivable grades of domestic service, boys as helpers at stables or pot-boys. Others were apprenticed to trades, many to bakers and weavers, but the commonest trades for boys seem to have been tailoring and shoemaking. There were also trades so unprofitable or disagreeable that only parish children or the children of the very poor were apprenticed to them. All, though, shared the common fate of being wholly at the whim and temper of their employers.'

The duties of a 'soap boy' were to heat the water his master used for shaving, to fill the soap bowls, to sweep hair from the floor, and generally to do as he was told; the slightest infringement would earn him a beating. Most soap boys were made to sleep on their employer's premises and were fed with the scraps from his table.

There is evidence that the first boy employed by Todd was a teenager named Thomas Simpkins. The confirmation of this is to be found in a poignant little document discovered among the Demon Barber's effects after his arrest. It takes the form of a bill from the Peckham Rye Asylum to which Todd appears to have confined the boy at some period in 1786. It seems hard to believe the reason for this incarceration was madness on the boys' part, and I suspect that he had become the first to realise just what Sweeney Todd was doing to his unsuspecting clients.

The document reads: 'Mr Sweeney Todd, Fleet Street, London. Paid one year's keep and burial of Thomas Simpkins, aged fifteen. Found dead in his bed after residing at the asylum ten months and four days.'

The various fictional accounts of Sweeney Todd's life make much of his ill-treatment of his various apprentices, but actual details about the boys, their names, ages and where they came from are scant. Understandably, with no one to turn to and the ever-present threat of a beating — worse still, to be turned out onto the streets again — most kept their silence: a silence they were to carry to their unknown graves.

The second murder which can with some confidence be ascribed to Sweeney Todd was, like the earlier one at Hyde Park Corner, committed in the street. In fact, the evidence points to the conclusion that it was to be some months — perhaps even a year or more — before the Demon Barber began regularly robbing and killing behind his own shop door.

This new crime was every bit as audacious as the first, and can be seen to bear the barber's hallmarks though, as before, he is not named in the newspaper account of the murder. The clipping is taken from the *Daily Courant* of 14 April, 1785:

A CUT-THROAT BARBER

A horrid murder has been committed in Fleet Street on the person of a young gentleman from the country while on a visit to relatives in London.

During the course of a walk through the city, he chanced to stop to admire the striking clock of St Dunstan's Church and there fell into conversation with a man in the clothing of a barber.

> *The two men came to an argument, and of a sudden the*
> *barber took from his clothing a razor and slit the throat of*
> *the young man, thereafter disappearing into the alleyway*
> *of Hen and Chicken Court and was seen no more.*

The locality is, of course, right next door to Sweeney Todd's shop, and one can only wonder today why — on the strength of the identification — the barber was not one of the first people to be questioned by the law. But we are talking about very different times and a very different law enforcement agency — of which more anon.

An apprentice was also killed by Todd at around this same time, though not a boy in his employment. According to a certain Arabella Wilmot who is quoted in the Charles Fox version of our subject's life, the barber was the last person known to have seen alive a boy who worked for her family.

'A short time ago,' she stated, 'an apprentice in the service of my father was sent to the West End to receive a considerable sum of money. He never returned with it, and from that day to this we have heard nothing of him, although from inquiries my father made he ascertained that the apprentice had received the money. He was last seen parting from a friend at the Corner of Milford Lane, saying that he intended to call upon Sweeney Todd the barber to have his hair cut. My father later called upon this Sweeney Todd who indignantly denied that such a person had ever called at his shop.

'A reward was offered to anyone who could provide information regarding the boy's fate, but no clue whatever could be obtained. Not even the remotest trace was found of the poor lad and his disappearance remains a mystery,' she added.

This killing — if we are satisfied that Todd was the murderer — was the first in which he made financial gain. It was also to provide the pattern which most of his later crimes would follow: that of the customer who entered his shop never to be seen again.

The death shortly after this of a pawnbroker named Joseph Hansbury is also attributed to Todd. Rumour said that the barber had visited the man's premises nearby in The Strand on a number of occasions to shave him, and that he had been there just a few hours before Hansbury's body was found, his throat cut, lying in a pool of blood in one of the upstairs rooms above the shop. The coroner, however, returned a verdict of 'temporary insanity' and the pawnbroker was buried without further ceremony.

A somewhat shady dealer in stocks, bonds and lottery shares at the Royal Exchange named Rheuben Marney also suffered the same fate. He, too, was believed to have conducted some business with the Fleet Street barber, and was found in his place of business with his throat open from ear to ear. But once again apparently no attempt was made to interrogate Todd according to the available evidence.

Only one more victim is believed to have been murdered by Sweeney Todd beyond the confines of his shop — a man named Tony Thong, a petty crook and embezzler whose body was found in Fleur-de-Lis Court. A description of his death (also from the pages of the *Daily Courant*) indicates that his end was brutal in the extreme.

'The throat had been slashed with a razor from one side of the neck to the other. The skull, too, was crushed in, and the brain had gushed out as a sharp implement had entered the head, and lay in thick clots, matting the surrounding hair together in clammy flakes.

'Blood had also oozed from the mouth and ears, and, in addition to all this, the spine was completely broken, as was evident from the way in which the dead man was doubled up, the back of his head and his heels being nearly together.'

According to gossip once again, Thong was said to have been seen in conversation with Sweeney Todd several times in the public house which gave its name to the Court; but there were no friends or relatives to pursue any inquiries and the hapless Thong was soon after confined to a pauper's grave.

Although, as we have seen, crime was rampant throughout London in 1785–6, this spate of murders in the neighbourhood of Fleet Street gave rise to the suggestion that a 'Human Ghoul' was preying on the vicinity: a kind of forerunner to the Victorian era's infamous 'Jack the Ripper'. Certainly there is circumstantial evidence of this name being bandied about in local gossip, but unfortunately there are no actual newspaper accounts which might be helpful in linking it to the deaths ascribed to Sweeney Todd. In fact, Todd may well not have been the 'Human Ghoul' of rumour at all — but the trail of death he had already left would certainly have qualified him for the epithet. The gossip might also have served as a warning to him that he was running an ever increasing risk of discovery killing this way in public view.

Whether this surmise is true or not, there is no doubt that Sweeney Todd never again murdered one of his victims in their homes or on the streets of London. In fact, the indications are clear that by now he had the wherewithal to kill and rob with greater certainty and security on his own premises. Sweeney Todd was now in possession of his infamous revolving chair.

8

A Victim of the Fatal Chair

There is only one authentic account of a victim being murdered in Sweeney Todd's revolving chair, although all the fictional lives and stage dramas about the Demon Barber contain their own colourful versions. The report in question, which I have endeavoured to reconstruct in the following pages, was made by a London night-watchman whose father had been killed by Sweeney Todd around the year 1798.

The authenticity for this report is to be found in a book entitled of *A Gothic Biography* by Montague Summers, a mammoth and painstaking study of macabre literature and its origins published in 1940. Summers, a Roman Catholic priest, spent years investigating the legend of Sweeney Todd, in literature, plays and reality, and concluded in his work:

'It has been denied that there was any such barber's shop in Fleet Street and the idea that Sweeney Todd has a real original has been scouted, a little rashly it would seem, for the authors of these works were drawing upon a long-standing and obstinate, if possibly only an oral authority, since there persisted a very old Fleet Street tavern tradition (current before 1800) that such an individual as Sweeney Todd existed, and his story is only a little exaggerated.

'This may well be the case,' Summers continues, 'as curiously crimes have an odd habit of repeating themselves in various countries even in detail. The old watchman, outside the gate of St Bartholomew's Hospital, used to aver that his father had been murdered for his coin by Sweeney Todd about 1798.'

There are few hospitals in London with a more fascinating

history than St Bartholomew's Hospital situated in West Smith-field, a few yards from Newgate Street. Founded in the Middle Ages, it rose to pre-eminence in the medical field despite the bizarre theories of some of its early physicians. Notable among these was John of Gaddesden, the court physician to Edward II, who apparently advised in cases of smallpox that the patient should be wrapped in red and everything about him had to be the same colour! He also prescribed for a disease of the body known as stone, which hardened the skin, a plaster of dung and a mixture of headless crickets and beetles to be rubbed over the affected parts.

Barts Hospital was another London building to benefit from the will of the Lord Mayor of London, Sir Richard Whittington, although the major reconstruction work on the property did not take place until the eighteenth century when the familiar quadrangle structure was built. A laboratory was also added in 1793. This same era saw the presentation to the hospital of two paintings by Hogarth based on patients he had studied in the hospital, 'The Pool of Bethesda' and 'The Good Samaritans', both of which still hang in the building today.

Though long famous for its care of the poor of London, night-watchmen were still necessary to guard the premises after darkness, especially because of its proximity to Newgate Prison. In the later half of the eighteenth century, a number of hand-picked men were employed in this capacity. One of their small number was John Shadwell, the man whose father's throat had been cut by Sweeney Todd. The older Shadwell had been one of the seven Beadles employed by the hospital as a petty officer responsible for keeping law and order; and he had been able to use his position to secure his son work on the staff.

Shadwell's account of his father's murder has survived in an incomplete handwritten document and in the oral traditions of West Smithfield, to which Montague Summers referred. I have here, though, attempted to put the facts together into narrative form.

* * *

It was a dark, rainy afternoon in late autumn as Thomas Shadwell made his way along Fleet Street to his job as a Beadle at St Bartholomew's Hospital. He lived in Covent Garden and normally walked the mile from his home by way of Temple Bar, down Fleet Street and Farringdon Street, and then up Snow Hill to the hospital. Normally he worked during the day; but the rising tide of crime in the city of late had made the hospital authorities concerned for security and they had instructed Shadwell to be doubly vigilant. He had therefore decided to work the occasional night shift.

Shadwell was a comfortably-off man, and took pride in his job and his appearance. He wore with pride the three-cornered hat and cloak of his office which was provided by St Bartholomew's and he was always well turned out and clean shaven. In his pockets he always kept some change for a drink on his way home.

This day, however, his beard was feeling decidedly rough and he decided to have a shave before starting work. He had passed the shop with 'Sweeney Todd, Barber' over the door many times, but never ventured inside. Previously he had always gone to a barber he knew in Drury Lane, but today he felt like a change. It was to prove a fatal mistake.

As he neared Temple Bar, Shadwell became aware of how few people were about. Those like him who had to brave the elements were pressing as close to the buildings as they could to escape the worst of the weather. Although it was not yet quite five o'clock, the general gloom made it seem like evening already. It was going to be a long, wet night, Thomas Shadwell thought.

Lights were visible in the windows of most of the taverns and shops he passed, but it was only when a door was hastily opened by someone going in or out that any flash of colour and warmth illuminated the road outside.

In the downpour, the outlines of the buildings all around seemed indistinct, and the few people about huddled shapelessly into their clothes as they hurried by. There was not much traffic, either, and even the usual street sellers who peddled their wares had disappeared into the alleyways or taverns.

Shadwell paused just as he reached St Dunstan's Church. A

whirring sound had caught his ear, and as his eyes glanced upwards at the big clock projecting from the side of the church, he saw the hour was just about to strike. For a moment there was stillness and then two small doors opened beside the clock face. A pair of gold-painted figures emerged, their heads moving from side to side. With mechanical efficiency they struck five blows on the bells suspended between them. Shadwell allowed the rain to drizzle onto his face as he watched. The sight of the clock in operation never failed to impress him, though he must have seen it a thousand times.

It was the flash of something from the nearby window of a shop which disturbed his thoughts. A flash of something silver illuminated by an oil lamp. It had come from the window of 'Sweeney Todd, Barber'.

The shop was pretty dark and evil-looking, Shadwell had decided on past occasions as he walked by; and on a day like this with the overhanging gables throwing everything beneath into even deeper shadows, it looked, if anything, more sinister still.

The Beadle ran his hand over his chin. It was definitely heavy with stubble: he couldn't turn up for work like this. He shrugged. What shop in this grimy city didn't look the worse for wear after some of the bad winters there had been recently? he thought.

Shadwell made up his mind. He pushed open the door and walked into the barber's shop.

The man he saw standing inside in the feeble glow of a pair of oil lamps seemed very much what one would expect from the outside of his premises. He was heavily-built, had small, glinting eyes and a mouth with a rather unpleasant droop to it. His hair grew thickly on his head, and behind both ears he had a pair of combs. His hands were large, and his finger nails rather dirty. When the man smiled his ingratiating smile it became something akin to a squint.

For a moment, Thomas Shadwell stood rooted to the spot. The barber put down the razor he had been stropping and crossed the room to his side. Todd indicated the big wooden chair standing in the centre of the shop.

'Is it a shave you require, sir?' he said. 'Sit down. I'll soon polish you off.'

Shadwell then became aware of another, smaller, figure standing in the gloom. He made out the features of a young boy wearing an apron similar to that of the barber. He was obviously the man's 'soap boy'.

As if suddenly becoming aware of the boy, too, the barber spoke to him. 'Now, lad, I've just realised the time. I want you to hurry off and fetch me some fish for my tea while I attend to this gentleman. Here is the money. Now be off with you.'

The boy seemed to hesitate momentarily before taking the two coins from his master's outstretched hand. But once he had taken them, he hurried out of the front door without a backward glance.

Shadwell felt just the smallest twinge of unease as he allowed himself to be led to the chair: it was made of very sturdy wood, he thought, and he wondered why it was set in the centre of the room so far away from the table on which the barber kept his soap bowls and razors.

As he took off his cloak and hat and handed them to the barber whom he assumed must be the curiously named Sweeney Todd, Shadwell was conscious of the rain beating with increasing force against the window and the sound of some rusty hinges swinging to and fro outside.

'What a day it is, Mr Todd,' he said. 'I hope you have a steady hand.'

'Oh, don't be afraid of that, my dear sir,' the barber replied with something close to a smirk on his face. 'My hand is as steady as it was twenty years ago when I was a boy. The elements have no effect upon me, I assure you!'

At this he gave a sinister, rather mirthless laugh which made the hairs on the back of Thomas Shadwell's neck stand up.

'Do seat yourself comfortably, sir,' Sweeney Todd continued, taking down one of his Magnum Bonum razors and strapping it carefully on the belt hanging beside the fireplace.

As he settled back in the chair, Shadwell was conscious of a smell — a rather unpleasant smell. He was just about to sniff again, when the barber spoke.

'I have not seen you before, sir,' the tradesman said, finishing his stropping and now poised above his customer. 'I can see you are a man of distinction. A Beadle, too.'

'Indeed,' Shadwell replied. 'I am employed by St Bartholomew's Hospital. A fine hospital. Do you know it?'

'I have not had the need of its services,' the barber grinned his evil grin again, 'but I have heard good reports. You have an important position there?'

Shadwell could not resist preening himself.

'I am the most senior of the Beadles,' he said. 'Thirty years service. This fine timepiece was given to me only last year.'

The Beadle put his hand into his pocket and withdrew a gold watch on a chain that glinted in the light of the oil lamp. Some coins also jingled in his pocket as he moved.

'A fine piece. A fine piece, *indeed*,' the barber said, the gleam in his eyes hidden as he moved around to the back of the chair. Then:

'Oh, pardon me, sir. What am I thinking of. About to shave you without hot water! Do excuse me a moment while I go to my back room for a bowl and some more clean towels.'

Sweeney Todd instantly left the room. Shadwell allowed his eyes to roam around the place. It did not look as if it had been properly cleaned for years. Should he take this moment to get up and leave before this unsavoury man got to work on him? Polish him off, hadn't he said. After all, why should he pay to be frightened half to death?

The Beadle's thoughts were suddenly interrupted by a sound from the back room where the barber had disappeared. It sounded like the noise of a heavy bolt being drawn, followed by a noise of creaking that seemed to come from beneath his feet.

Before the startled man could even move, however, he felt the chair beneath him begin to tip backwards. The floorboards in front of his feet also started to rise up in front of his startled eyes, and an involuntary cry sprang from the lips. Then the ceiling seemed to spin before the Beadle's eyes and the last thing Thomas Shadwell ever felt was falling backwards out of his chair and plunging down, down into a stygian darkness ...

Scarcely had the victim of Sweeney Todd's chair struck the floor of the cellar below with a sickening crunch and lapsed into instant unconsciousness, than another chair had revolved noiselessly to take the place of the original.

From behind the door, the Demon Barber peered into the room to assure himself that everything was as it should be. The shaving chair was once more empty awaiting the next customer.

Sweeney Todd selected another Magnum Bonum from the rack on the wall and began to descend the stairs to his cellar.

'Another rich one for the picking,' he smirked to himself. 'See how I polish 'em off!'

* * *

The murder of the Beadle Thomas Shadwell remained undiscovered for two years until Sweeney Todd was finally arrested. The crime was not detected sooner not least because Shadwell had never used the barber's shop before and had never given anyone a clue that he might do so. Shadwell's son was sure his father had died in the barber's infamous chair because the old man's watch, his pride and joy, was later recovered from a cupboard at 186 Fleet Street. But of Shadwell himself not so much as a hair from his head was ever found.

There have been several suggestions as to how Sweeney Todd devised his 'fiendish weapon of death' as the shaving chair has been described. One unlikely account appeared in a leaflet, *Sweeney Todd, The Demon Barber*, written by Felix McGlennon in 1911.

'A conversation with a skilful mechanic gave him the idea of the trap-door,' McGlennon's account claims, 'which they made between them. And when it was completed Sweeney tested its efficiency upon the unsuspecting mechanic, and thereby became the sole possessor of the secret.'

This is not a theory which matches the facts, however. According to John Shadwell, when Todd was arrested he claimed to

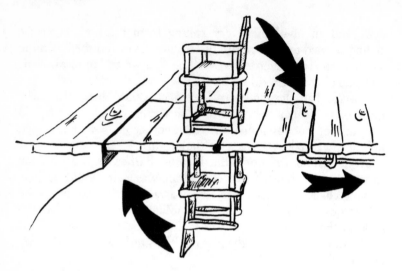

The secret of Sweeney Todd's deadly revolving chair.

have invented the chair himself, utilising the skills of basic lever-age which he had learned while apprenticed to the culter: the purpose of the movable chairs, Todd claimed, was no more sinister than to allow him to easily tip away hair clippings and similar debris from his work directly into the cellar below!

As the diagram here shows, the apparatus actually consisted of two chairs fixed onto opposite sides of a square section of floor-boards pivoted in the middle. A movable bolt fitted beneath the edge of these boards was joined by a system of rods to a small lever behind the rear door of the shop. By pulling this lever, the rods withdrew the bolt and the weight of the customer leaning back in the chair was sufficient to cause the contrivance to turn through forty-five degrees, so depositing the victim onto the stone floor below and the lower chair up into the shop. By returning the bolt to its former position, the chair was once more securely in place until required again.

The system was, in fact, simplicity itself — but deadly efficient.

Another statement Felix McGlennon made about the *modus operandi* of the Demon Barber is more accurate.

'Sweeney Todd made the discovery, perhaps by accident, that beneath his shop and the adjoining church were extensive underground passages and vaults stretching away in various directions, which few people had ever heard of or suspected to exist.

'Using the chairs he worked cautiously, murdering many, and grew rich, but the disposal of the bodies troubled him, as he had to bury them beneath the stones underground,' the report adds.

Sweeney Todd was certainly an ingenious and vengeful man; but he was also greedy and cunning. Not satisfied with the money and valuables he had already amassed, the barber sought for a better means of disposing of the troublesome bodies of his victims. He found the solution with the help of a woman whose name and gruesome reputation is now as much a part of the legend of the Demon Barber as his own.

9

The Secret of the Meat Pies

Not every customer that Sweeney Todd dispatched into his cellar died immediately they struck the ground. According to the *Gentleman's Magazine* version of his life, the chair killed outright five out of every seven victims, breaking their necks as they fell backwards onto the stone floor. The remaining few who showed any signs of life after their fall, Todd had to 'polish off' by cutting their throats. The Demon Barber was always quick to inspect any body immediately after he had made sure that the chair was back in place. He would then slice through the jugular of his victim with practised ease.

The one problem that always remained after robbing the corpse was to dispose of it. Initially, there had been space in the underground vaults beneath the church which adjoined his cellar. But as the numbers mounted — and the work of burying the bodies became increasingly arduous — the killer sought for an easier alternative.

C. W. Biller, the author of *The Story of Sweeney Todd*, published in 1924, provides the basic details of the solution he found.

'Sweeney Todd had been intimate with a Mrs Lovett for some time when he discovered that a passage could be made to communicate with a shop in Bell Yard, and he installed her in it as an expert pie maker. Then the horrible idea occurred to him that it would be both profitable and expedient if she used the flesh of the dead for her pies, and if any of their assistants suspected anything — they, too, became pie fillings.'

Bell Yard, like Fleet Street, also enjoyed a notorious reputation at this period in history. Sir John Fortescue, the friend of the poet Alexander Pope, who once lived in a house in the cramped little passageway, referred to it derisively as 'that filthy old place'. Nonetheless, it obviously had a kind of charm and atmosphere of its own — an atmosphere which appealed to Charles Dickens, for one, because he placed part of his novel *Bleak House* (1852–3) in the vicinity. Today, Bell Yard is a little haven of quiet running between the bustle of The Strand alongside the Royal Courts of Justice to Carey Street.

The information we possess about the Mrs Lovett who became Sweeney Todd's accomplice in crime varies considerably in the different versions of the legend. Some describe her as a middle-aged woman, rather plain, with a cold and uncomfortable smile; while others, like the C. Arthur Pearson (1949), present her as little short of a beauty:

'She was tall and slender with a mass of dark curling hair and the golden, peachlike complexion of the true brunette. Her lips were vividly crimson, her long heavily lashed eyes of a dark green hazel, flecked near the pupils with little specks of gold. She carried herself with the half insolent air of one who was fully aware of the value of her own beauty, and her voice when she spoke matched her appearance and possessed a surprisingly cultured accent.'

If, as I suspect, this account rather over-glamourises Mrs Lovett, there is still plenty of evidence that she was attractive to men. For there had been more than one man in her life before Sweeney Todd appeared and changed her existence for ever.

The suggestion has been put forward that she had a penchant for strong, even violent men, and that this was the basis of her relationship with the barber. Yet just how she fell in with his appalling plan to use the bodies of his victims as filling for her pies is still a matter of debate.

There is also some disagreement among those who have studied the legend as to whether her Christian name was Margery or Sarah, as both appear in the various version of the story. As Margery is the most frequently used, it is the one I have settled for in these pages.

Mrs Lovett was apparently born in London, although nothing

is known of her early history. In her teens she married a baker named Joe Lovett and for some years the pair ran a business in Holborn. After her husband's sudden and unexpected death, she is believed to have lived with a 'Major Barnet' until he was proved to be a fraud and had to flee the city. She was then for a time the mistress of a city merchant who installed her in a house in Covent Garden.

Her first meeting with Sweeney Todd is said to have taken place a few years after he had settled in Fleet Street when his nefarious activities had already made him quite wealthy. Still anxious to make more money, he was always on the look-out for new opportunities and apparently sensed something of a kindred spirit in Mrs Lovett's calculating eyes. The attraction between the big, ugly man and the buxom young widow was also, without doubt, strongly sexual.

The Charles Fox version of the Sweeney Todd story also confirms that the barber was the owner of Mrs Lovett's pie shop in Bell Yard.

'Sweeney Todd felt himself quite at home in Bell Yard,' the narrative states. 'He was, in truth, the landlord of Mrs Lovett's house. It had not been safe to make the extensive underground alterations in the place if Mrs Lovett had been the tenant of a stranger, so Sweeney had purchased the freehold.'

Felix McGlennon adds a little further interesting information about the nature of their relationship.

'Mrs Lovett was his mistress and partner in crime, but no one ever saw them together, for they met by means of mysterious underground passageways entirely unknown to the outside world. By a passage known only to himself and his paramour, Sweeney Todd could make his way towards the pie shop, and manipulating a secret spring he caused the wall to open like a door so he could enter the bakehouse.'

It was not uncommon in London in the eighteenth century for bakeries to be situated in the cellars of bread and pastry shops. A contemporary description of an establishment which was probably very similar to that of Mrs Lovett's, describes such underground bakeries as having rough red tiles on the floor and pieces of flint and ragged stones hammered into the earthen walls to reinforce them. Extra strength was provided by beams of timber in the ceiling propped up by wooden pillars set into the floor. A large furnace provided the heat for the ovens to cook the trays of pies, which were normally made in batches of a hundred. Once cooked, the pies would be transported to the shop above on a movable platform raised by a series of pulleys.

Thomas Peckett Prest, who wrote his version of the legend only a few years after the events, actually worked in Fleet Street and was familiar with Bell Yard. His description of Mrs Lovett's pie shop and its customers — predominantly clerks and lawyers from Lincoln's Inn and Grays Inn as well as employees of the legal profession from Chancery Lane and Holborn – can be taken as accurate and authentic.

'On the left hand side of Bell Yard, going down from Carey Street, was, at the time we write of, one of the most celebrated shops for the sale of veal and pork pies that ever London produced. High and low, rich and poor, resorted to it; its fame had spread far and wide; and at twelve o'clock every day when the first batch of pies was sold there was a tremendous rush to obtain them.

'Their fame had spread great distances, some even carried them into the country as a treat to their friends. Oh, those delicious pies! There was about them a flavour never surpassed and rarely equalled; the paste was of the most delicate construction, and impregnated with the aroma of delicious gravy that defied description; the fat and the lean meat were also so artistically mixed.'

The counter in Mrs Lovett's shop was horseshoe-shaped and it was the habit of some of the customers to sit around this while they ate and exchanged banter. Some were even said to have flirted with the owner, but her only encouragement had been to urge those who had any money left to buy more pies. There were those among her customers who said that her smile was only on her lips and not from her heart. She was a deceiver, a woman with a secret. Margery Lovett only had eyes for business, they maintained.

Certainly Mrs Lovett made good use of the money that came into her possession. Her love of expensive items inspired her to furnish the upper rooms of the shop with fine furniture and carpets, and it was whispered that her bed was covered with silken sheets. The irony of making love on the very material that had helped support his family would probably not have been lost on Sweeney Todd.

After their moments of intimacy — which legend tells us followed a successful murder and the preparation of the flesh for the meat pies — Mrs Lovett may well have found her lover's general coarseness and lack of education irritating. Indeed, she more than once complained about Todd's 'greed for money' when they already had more than enough to satisfy their needs. Margery Lovett considered herself an educated and clever woman and desperately wanted to broaden her knowledge of art and literature. She was, as another contemporary report put it, 'no common, everyday sort of woman'.

The Demon Barber, on the other hand, simply wanted to satisfy his lust and his passion for money.

* * *

Sweeney Todd's skill at cutting up and dismembering the bodies of his victims has never been in question. He had learned the basic skills of the 'barber surgeon' from his first instructor, Plummer, and in the cellar beneath the shop perfected his ability with the regular practice each of his victims provided.

The speed with which the Demon Barber dismembered his victims before *rigor mortis* could set in and make his job so much more difficult says a lot about his expertise at this grim task. He had to work in the claustrophobic conditions of the tiny cellar with only a wax candle to provide illuminations. With the amount of blood that must have spilled from the corpses onto the cellar floor, it is not difficult to imagine how slippery and unpleasant the whole place must have become. Sweeney Todd, apparently, never let such inconveniences bother him.

Once the bodies had been stripped of their clothes, Todd would butcher off the arms and legs and then slice the soft flesh from the torso. This would be added to the 'meat' stripped from

A fanciful nineteenth-century engraving of a handsome Sweeney Todd 'polishing off' a female victim.

the limbs plus the heart, liver and kidneys, and put in a box for carrying to Mrs Lovett's underground bakery. When he had separated up all the flesh that might be edible, he would make a separate pile of the bones and then carry them off into the adjacent vaults for disposal. In carrying out this part of his mission, the killer only had the light of his wax candle to guide him along the narrow passageways. Later evidence was to reveal that he had carefully picked a vault to hide the bones in which belonged to a local family named Weston whose line had many years earlier become extinct. It was one vault that was unlikely ever to be disturbed. There is a possibility that some of the other family tombs beneath St Dunstan's were used for this purpose, but only one description has survived of what was found in the Weston vault. It does not make pleasant reading.

'Piled one upon each other on the floor and reaching half way up to the ceiling, lay a decomposing mass of human remains,' the report from the *Courier* says. 'Heaped one upon another, heedlessly tossed into the disgusting heap any way, lay pieces of gaunt skeletons with pieces of flesh here and there only adhering to the bones. Heads in a similar state of decay were tumbled about, the whole enough to strike such horror into the heart of any man.'

Successfully having concealed the bones in the vault, Sweeney Todd then carried the flesh along to Mrs Lovett's bakehouse, where it would be turned into the meat pies which she sold to her unsuspecting customers.

The various accounts of the Demon Barber's life are uncertain as to whether Mrs Lovett was solely responsible for preparing the pies. It is difficult to believe that she could have coped with her extensive clientele on her own; and one must not forget the claim in C. W. Biller's account written in 1924 that if any of the couple's 'assistants' suspected what was going on, 'they, too, became pie fillings'.

There is some evidence that Mrs Lovett employed a young girl to help her serve in the shop. Several of the fictionalised biographies also claim that she employed a pie-maker in the underground kitchen below. This is certainly feasible; and it is not beyond the realms of possibility that an uneducated man would have been unable to tell the difference between animal meat and that of human beings which had been sufficiently carved up. What makes it difficult to sustain this hypothesis is the complete absence of such a witness at the subsequent trial of Sweeney Todd. This, though, did not prevent the early chroniclers of the legend from introducing a cook who prepared the 'cannibal pies'. The anonymous author of *A Life of Sweeney Todd* (1897) even turned the pie-maker into the hero of his account as the man who ultimately exposed Mrs Lovett's evil trade.

'There was an awful stillness in the shop,' he writes, 'and all eyes were fixed upon Mrs Lovett and the cavity through which the next batch of those delicious pies were coming. The platform could be heard to be making its way upwards by means of a ratchet-wheel and catch.

'For a moment Mrs Lovett paused to take breath. The load seemed heavier than usual, she thought, or else her nerves were beginning to fail her. She began to turn the windlass again. At last the tops of the pies appeared.

'Those clustered in the shop saw the rim of the large tray, and just as the platform was level with the floor, up flew the trays and pies, as if something had exploded beneath them. A tall, slim man sprang out of the shaft and onto the counter.

'It was the cook who, from the cellar beneath, had laid himself as flat as he could beneath the tray of pies and so had been worked up to Mrs Lovett's shop.

' "Gentlemen," he cried, " I am Mrs Lovett's cook. The pies are made of *human flesh*!" '

Such a scene obviously made an ideal cliff-hanger for a Victorian penny dreadful, but the manner in which the conspiracy between the pie-maker and the Demon Barber was actually revealed began much more prosaically than that. The credit, in fact, belongs to an unpleasant smell and the relentless pursuit of a Bow Street Runner who picked up the scent.

10

The Bow Street Runners on the Scent

In the middle of the eighteenth century the state of law enforcement, such as it was, meant that the clever criminal in London had a very good chance of escaping detection — not just once, but as often as his wits and ingenuity would allow him to keep one step ahead of those who represented the law.

It is a curious fact of British history that the people of these islands steadfastly rejected the idea of a 'police force' for generations. While every other country in Europe had its own professional law agencies, the very idea of the term police — a French word that first came into common usage in 1714 — seemed to Britons a threat to their freedom and individual liberties.

Across the Channel, the French had had a police force as long as their standing army. Both were expected to guard the frontiers against invasion; but when no such danger threatened, these 'police' men were expected to enforce the domestic laws. Not surprisingly, they were known as *gens d'armes* (men of arms) or *gendarmes*. Oliver Cromwell had actually made an attempt to introduce such a force in England — but it was at a time when his grip on the nation was slipping and the plan came to nothing. The whole concept seemed somehow 'un-English'. Even though highwaymen were robbing travellers on the country roads with seeming impunity, and burglars and footpads plagued those who lived in the towns and cities, still the business of enforcing the law was left almost solely to private enterprise. Those members of the public who did complain to the Houses of Parliament about the lawlessness of the country were brushed aside with the reply that it was the responsibility of the various country districts (the 'hundreds' which have since become modern parishes) to administer justice. In any event, they argued, it would be so costly to the exchequer to set up a professional force that it might well ruin the economy.

In effect, every man had to be his own policeman. Any person who was robbed was expected to raise the hue and cry and try to catch the criminal himself. If he was successful and wished to prosecute, he had to do so at his own expense. Small wonder that if the amount stolen was small or the criminal seemed a dangerous villain, few members of the public were prepared to play amateur detective.

Many of the officials of the hundreds had, however, made some kind of an attempt to preserve law and order by appointing parish constables, whose assistance any aggrieved person might enlist. But these men were all amateurs, doing their police work in their spare time: that many of them tackled the job with less than enthusiasm may be gauged by the fact that the job was compulsory and unpaid — not unlike jury service today. The term of office of these constables was for one year, and there is plentiful evidence that many a tradesman saddled with the job would pay — or even coerce — an employee to serve in his place. All constables were, though, entitled to charge a member of the public for their services.

There was another layer of authority above parish constables: the magistrates. They were unpaid also, although they were allowed to keep certain of the fees and fines they imposed. These men could order arrests and examine prisoners before they were taken to court. Many sat as judge and jury on the bench, too.

In fact, it was only in London that there was anything approaching a 'police force' before the mid–1800s. These were the band of night-watchmen who had been established in the second half of the seventeenth century during the reign of Charles II. Nicknamed 'Charlies', the job of these men was to patrol the streets at night, armed with a cudgel and a rattle with which to attract attention when any crime was discovered. These ostensibly 'professional' policemen were paid one shilling per night. The basic flaw in this arrangement was that the watchmen were mostly elderly men who had been unable to get work in the more strenuous professions: they were often scarcely able to lift a stick, let alone wield it! Consequently, most 'Charlies' were treated with brutality by the criminal fraternity if they interfered, and with scant regard by the general public.

In 1749, however, just seven years before Sweeney Todd was born, the first serious attempt to combat crime in London was initiated with the founding of the Bow Street Runners, Britain's first police-detectives. This famous band of men to whom we owe the modern Metropolitan Police Force, came into existence thanks to an unpaid Westminster magistrate named Colonel Thomas de Veil. Though not above taking bribes to line his own pocket, de Veil was a brave and energetic man who, without any assistance, carried out his own detective work to bring a large number of criminals to justice. At the end of his career he claimed, perhaps somewhat exaggeratedly, to have 'executed or transported over 1,900 of the greatest malefactors that ever appeared in England'.

De Veil's pioneer work was taken up by Henry Fielding, the novelist and author if *Tom Jones* (1749), who, uncertain of his success as a writer and anxious to secure the future for his family, accepted a magistrate's job with an annual guarantee of perks worth £1,000. Having weighed up the size of the problem he had inherited from de Veil, Fielding managed to persuade a group of six 'honest and true' former parish constables to band together and clear the London streets of criminals. Though he was in no position to offer them a salary, he would ensure the six received any rewards on offer.

Fired on by Fielding's own enthusiasm, these men — 'Mr Fielding's People' as they were first called — took to the streets to wage war on crime. Within two years, their number had risen to eighty and they were being called the Bow Street Runners, after the house in Bow Street where their chief lived.

The public were not charged for asking the Runners to investigate a crime, and everyone was encouraged to report cases of

*Sweeney Todd's World: Late 18th Century
London as depicted by Hogarth.*

Temple Bar in 1761 and the site today,
now occupied by The Griffin.

SWEENEY TODD

THE BARBER OF FLEET St.

A rare portrait of Sweeney Todd sold at the time of his trial in 1802.

The site of Sweeney Todd's shop. It was located in the extreme right hand corner of this 1780 picture of St Dunstan's church.

The same spot today.

A contemporary engraving said to be of Mrs Lovett – the notorious pie-maker of Bell Yard.

Bell Yard in 1761 and today. Mrs Lovett's pie shop stood approximately on the site now occupied by Butterworth's publishers.

A typical passageway and cavern of the type that have been found beneath Fleet Street.

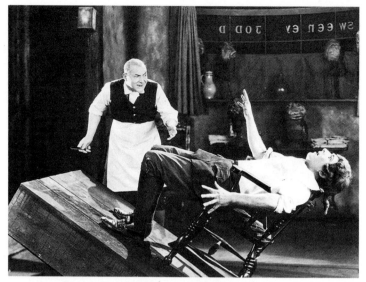

*Moore Marriott in the 1926 silent film version
of Sweeney Todd.*

*Denis Quilley and
Sheila Hancock
starred in Stephen
Sondheim's musical
thriller, **Sweeney
Todd,** which made
its debut on the
London stage
in 1980.*

law-breaking to Bow Street. Tragically — and with his plans working so well — Henry Fielding died in 1754; but his place was at once taken by his equally-dedicated half-brother, John. John Fielding went on to expand the force with foot patrols; open a criminal records office; and launch a weekly journal of news and information about crime, *Hue and Cry*, which would later become the famous *Police Gazette*. He also gave the Runners their famous motto, 'Quick Notice and Sudden Pursuit'.

By 1792 the Bow Street Runners had a total of eight offices in the city, each with three salaried police-magistrates and six detective officers. The Runners were paid a salary of 25 shillings per week which served as a retaining fee: they also received a share in any reward when a criminal was caught and convicted. The best of these men might hope to earn several hundred pounds a year. Unlike the modern policeman, the Runners had no uniform — a state of affairs which did not change until 1805 when a standardised dress of blue coat and trousers, red waistcoat and black hat was chosen to make them look as little like soldiers as possible.

One of the busiest of these Bow Street Runner offices was situated at number 10 Craven Street, a major road just off The Strand running down to the banks of the Thames. The area of jurisdiction for this office extended from St James's Park to St Paul's Cathedral, and included the notorious Fleet Street.

It was to this office, and to its police-magistrate, Sir Richard Blunt, that the first stories of the unpleasant odour at St Dunstan's Church were conveyed in 1799. Thereby started the chain of events which would bring an end to Sweeney Todd's reign of terror.

* * *

Like the story of the Bow Street Runners themselves, there is very little factual evidence to draw upon about the career of Sir Richard Blunt. The Runners were disbanded in 1839; and when the Bow Street Police Office itself was moved in 1881, virtually all the official records of the men and their inaugural battle against crime were destroyed. The reason for this discarding of priceless information about the forerunners of a force that now prides itself on the care with which it treats all data and records is heart-breakingly simple. The documents were just not thought worth keeping. Certainly there are a few records about the Bow Street Runners to be found at Scotland Yard and in the Public Record Office; but all the day-to-day journals and lists of successful pursuits and prosecutions have long since gone. To some criminologists this has made the Runners seem more like characters from fiction than fact. But a real force they most definitely were. And according to a tribute in the *Courier*, Sir Richard Blunt was 'one of the most acute, active and personally daring of the magistrates of London'. A man known for the zeal with which he pursued all law-breakers.

Sir Richard came from a wealthy London banking family of Essex Street, a small turning to the left at the top of Fleet Street where it joins The Strand. He was a man who evidently believed strongly in the ideals of Henry Fielding and the Bow Street Runners and had been most happy to be recruited to their ranks. As a person of considerable private means, he had the time as well as the inclination to devote himself to detective work whenever a case worthy of his mettle arose. It seems highly likely that Blunt himself felt there must be more to the stories of a 'horrid smell' emanating from St Dunstan's Church than was first apparent. Reports about this had been brought to him by Mr Otton, the Beadle of St Dunstan's, who also served as the parish constable. An account which subsequently appeared in the *Courier* explains how the whole curious business began:

'The matter came to light when the pious pages of the frequenters of St Dunstan's Church began to perceive a strange and most abominable odour throughout that sacred edifice. It was in vain that old women who came to hear the sermons, although they were too deaf to catch a third part of them, brought smelling-bottles and other means of stifling their noses. Notwithstanding this, still the dreadful charnel-house sort of smell would make itself most painfully and disagreeably apparent.

'The regular preacher at St Dunstan's, the Reverend Joseph Stillingport, also smelt it while in the pulpit, and was seen to sneeze in the midst of a discourse, and to hold to his pious mouth a handkerchief, in which was some strong and pungent essence, for the purpose of trying to overcome the horrible effluvia.

'The organ-blower and the organ-player were also both nearly stiffled, for the offensive odour seemed to ascend to the upper part of the church, although those who sat in what may be called the pit by no means escaped it. The churchwardens also wore contorted countenances and were almost afraid to breathe.

'The only person who did not complain bitterly of the dreadful odour in St Dunstan's Church was an old woman who had been a pew-opener for many years. But it was said she had lost the facilities of her nose, which probably accounted for the circumstance.

'As might be supposed, from the fact that this sort of thing had gone on for a few months, it began to excite some attention with a view to a remedy. For in the great city of London a nuisance of any sort or description requires to become venerable by age before anyone thinks of removing it. The church-wardens also began to fear that some pestilential disease would be the result if they for any longer period of time put up with the horrible stench, and so began to institute enquiries about what could be done to obviate it.'

Constable Otton, in the best tradition of the Bow Street Runners, reported the matter to his chief. What puzzled him, he said, was that the smell reminded him of putrefying corpses; yet no one had been buried in the church for many years.

Richard Blunt's first action was to pay a visit to St Dunstan's with Constable Otton. There, armed with cloths soaked in vinegar for their noses, he and the constable explored both the main body of the church and the vaults below. The stench was certainly overpowering; but no matter where they looked, no immediate cause could be found. There were no signs of any vaults having been opened or any of the notorious sewers in the vicinity having burst. Sir Richard and his man left the church none the wiser.

Just when it seemed the source of the problem of the stench-ridden church might prove insoluable, a crucial piece of gossip from the same neighbourhood reached the magistrate. Again it was passed on by one of his constables and, although initially there was no suggestion the two events might be linked, it certainly opened up a new line of enquiry. The story concerned the barber at 186 Fleet Street — a man called Sweeney Todd. Apparently, according to local gossip, a number of customers, including several sea-faring men, had used the shop and then had never again been seen. Sir Richard had never been a man to jump to conclusions, but his instincts told him he might just be onto something.

Of course, in a sprawling metropolis like London, the coming and going of people was never easy to keep track of — certainly not that of seamen who were in and out of the port all the time. But the stories had a persistence about them; and there was something familiar to Sir Richard about the name Sweeney Todd — it was one of those unusual names that stuck in the mind.

Sir Richard, the evidence suggests, consulted the records of the Bow Street Runners, and there found that Todd had actually appeared before him in court. Although there is only one brief reference to this incident in a fictionalised version of Sweeney Todd's life, it has the ring of truth about it. It suggests an excellent reason why Blunt decided to initiate investigations into the barber, leading him eventually to link the events in Todd's shop with those in the church. The story is told in *Sweeney Todd* by James McDonald (1910).

'Some years earlier, a lady walking along Fleet Street was attracted by a pair of shoe-buckles, studded with imitation diamonds, which were being worn by Sweeney Todd. She screamed out and declared that they belonged to her husband, who had gone out one morning from his house in Fetter Lane to be shaved, but had never returned.

'After the lady had established the identity of Todd she instituted proceedings which came before Sir Richard Blunt. However, the buckles were of too common a kind for the lady to persevere in her statement, and Todd, who maintained the most imperturbable coolness throughout the affair, was, of course, discharged.

'The matter did though leave a suspicion in the magistrate's mind. Other affairs, however, of more immediate urgency occupied his time, but the report by the constable of the stories regarding Todd revived all his former feelings and made him believe sharp and prompt attention was called for.'

Despite the fact that there is no documentation to support this story, circumstantial evidence lends weight to it being possible. In any event, Sir Richard Blunt now ordered his men to keep a watch on Sweeney Todd's shop while he himself reported his suspicions to the Secretary of State. Following a meeting with the government minister, he was given permission to continue the surveillance of Todd and 'use what means might be necessary' to get to the bottom of the mystery.

The decision to post the Runners in premises opposite 186 Fleet Street paid dividends for Sir Richard when, in the ensuing months, reports reached his office of at least three customers entering the shop who had not been seen to leave. He ordered his men to enter the barber's shop with as many clients as possible to keep an eye on them. To hasten his inquiries before more lives were lost, Blunt decided to search the vaults of St Dunstan's once again, accompanied by a party of Bow Street Runners. He was growing ever more convinced that if Sweeney Todd *was* killing his customers and hiding the bodies, it had to be somewhere in the adjoining cellars of the church. What he found on this new expedition, however, opened up a new, totally unexpected and gruesome element to the unfolding drama.

In his search of the vaults, Sir Richard made use of a special walking stick he had had made some years before. Underneath its gold top, the stick concealed a small compass; and the magistrate made use of this in order to explore the maze of corridors and passageways which he and his men had been nervous about entering on their previous visit. With only the lights of their oil lamps to aid them, the little party stumbled upon the grave of the Weston family and its grisly remains of human bodies. Going further, following the unmistakable tracks of human footsteps in the dirt and rubble, the Runners suddenly found themselves at the back to Mrs Lovett's underground cookhouse. The blood-stained evidence which Sir Richard Blunt saw there confirmed a nightmare he had been reluctant to admit to himself: Sweeney Todd was not only a mass murderer, but he was getting rid of the evidence by turning it into meat pies.

The minds of the men who trudged back along those passage-ways to the church must have been full of a mixture of revulsion and horror. They were determined to bring to justice the man who could perpetrate such evil — and his partner, too.

The readings from his compass enabled the magistrate to decide without much difficulty that the shop of Sweeney Todd's accomplice was in Bell Yard. Two Runners were at once despat-ched to keep watch on these premises, too. Before the day was out, Sir Richard Blunt had on his desk a memorandum about Mrs Lovett and what details were known of her.

Although the magistrate was now satisfied in his own mind about the collusion between the barber and the pie-maker, he was still anxious for more specific evidence against Todd. The monster might have found an easy way of disposing of the bodies; but what was he doing with his victim's clothes and valuables? Sir Richard decided to send one of his men to search Sweeney Todd's premises. Several days passed before a suitable opportunity arose — but the wait was worth every minute. The Runner who gained access to the building found several cupboards full of clothing and a drawer packed with valuables. Taking details of the names and initials on some of the hats and gold watches, he hurried back with the information to Craven Street.

Sir Richard now acted quickly. Three of his most senior con-stables were sent off to Bell Yard with a warrant for Mrs Lovett's arrest. He and the remaining men set out for Fleet Street.

Some of the more colourful accounts of the story of the Demon Barber claim that when Mrs Lovett was arrested in her shop as she was serving a group of customers, such was the outcry that she had to be saved from being lynched.

'The people who were in the shop spread the news all over

the neighbourhood,' says the Charles Fox version, 'and the place was soon jammed up with a maddened mob. They poured in from Fleet Street and Carey Street determined to tear her to bits and hang her on the lamp post in the middle of Bell Yard.' The Bow Street Runners, however, as good as their name, were able to spirit Mrs Lovett out of the back of the house into a waiting coach and driver her speedily to Newgate.

The vivacious young widow was a shadow of her former self by the time she reached the great, grey prison. Her face was white and drawn, her eyes wild with fear. All her beauty and composure had drained away. To the men who sat silently on each side of her, she blurted out her confession. Sweeney Todd had been the murderer — she was just his accomplice. The Demon Barber was the man they should arrest. Neither man spoke a word of reply or comfort during the journey. Once inside the prison Mrs Lovett, her nerve gone, demanded to see the Governor. She wanted to make a statement, she said, she was not going to be blamed for everything.

A version of Mrs Lovett's confession, printed by the *London Chronicle*, is probably accurate in essence, although it does offer a slightly different version of certain elements in the story.

'Believing that I am on the edge of the grave, I, Margery Lovett make this statement.

'Sweeney Todd first conceived the idea of that mutual guilt which we have both since carried out. He bought the house in Bell Yard, as likewise in Fleet Street, and by his own exertions he excavated an underground connection between the two, mining right under St Dunstan's Church, and through the vault of that building.

'When he had completed all his arrangements he came to me and made his offer. But he did not tell me that these arrangements were then complete as that, he doubtless thought, would have placed him too much in my power in the event of my refusing to co-operate with him in his iniquity. He need not have given himself that amount of trouble — I was willing.

'The plan he proposed was that the pie-shop should be opened for the sole purpose of getting rid of the bodies of people whom he might think proper to murder in or under his shop. He said that, fearing nothing and believing nothing, he had come to the conclusion that money was the greatest thing to be desired in this world, inasmuch as to it he had found that all people bowed down.

'He said that after the murder of anyone, he would take the flesh from the bones quickly and convey it to the shelves of the bakehouse in Bell Yard, the pieces to be materials for the pies. Minor arrangements he left to me. He murdered many. The business went on and prospered and we both grew rich. This is how we fell to our present state.'

After she fell silent, Mrs Lovett was asked by the Governor of Newgate if she had anything further to add. Shaking her head, she only enquired if her confession would be used against Sweeney Todd as well as herself.

'Yes, it is strong corroboration of the evidence against him,' she was told, 'and, as such, if there had been any doubt, would have gone far towards making his conviction certain.'

Unaware that he already had the most crucial evidence against Sweeney Todd, Sir Richard Blunt and his men strode into 186 Fleet Street to write the last chapter in the bloody saga of the Demon Barber.

11

The Trial of the Age

Investigating gruesome crimes in London was not altogether new to the Bow Street Runners, but the men who went with Sir Richard Blunt to Sweeney Todd's barber shop in Fleet Street in October 1801 must have wondered quite what kind of cold-blooded killer they would find there: a man who could calmly cut up bodies and then see the remains made into meat pies for public consumption. Though some of the officers might have recalled a grisly case which had occurred earlier in the same year on 26 April. The event has been reported in the *Annual Register*.

'About 8 in the evening,' it began, 'a mob assembled before a house in Wych Street, formerly the Queen of Bohemia Tavern (but now supposed to be unoccupied), in consequence of some boys who had been at play in the passage declaring they saw some persons through the keyhole employed in cutting up human bodies. The mob having increased, at length broke into the house in which they found several human bodies partly dissected, one body of a man who appeared to have been not long dead, with that of an infant not four months old, untouched, and several tubs with human flesh, etc.

'The stench was so great that many were glad to return without viewing the disgusting scene, and many who went in were seized with sickness. Notwithstanding it was explained to the mob that the house had been for some time used as an anatomical theatre, they were so enraged as to proceed to destroy the house.

'But a party of Bow Street officers arriving, at length succeeded in restoring peace to the great satisfaction of the neighbourhood who had been much alarmed at the idea that the mob would in

The arrest and imprisonment of the Demon Barber generated enormous public excitement throughout London.

their rage set fire to the house. The surgeons who were in the house made their escape by a back way, leaving several of their instruments behind them.'

Nothing so dramatic happened when Sir Richard Blunt and his men burst in on Sweeney Todd. The group of officers apparently established that the barber was alone before entering the shop. The magistrate immediately instructed that the front door and passage to the rear were to be covered to prevent any possible escape. With the traditional Runners' cry of 'Clap the darbies on his wrists!' Sweeney Todd was seized and handcuffed before he could cry out or make a move. He stood, looking bewildered, as Sir Richard Blunt informed him he was being arrested for murder.

The available evidence suggests that Todd once again tried to brazen it out with the man he had confronted before in court. A claim in a colourful version of the legend that one of the Bow Street Runners suggested the Demon Barber should be fastened into his own revolving chair in order to extort a confession from him, may be dismissed as mere sensationalism. Another claim that he tried to break free of the arresting officers and threatened them with the razor hidden up his sleeve is as doubtful as a statement that he simply broke down and wept. All that is certain, however, is that Sweeney Todd was arrested and taken away by coach to Newgate. Unlike the arrest of Mrs Lovett, not a single member of the public knew about the seizure of the barber until he was safely behind bars.

The news of Mrs Lovett's confession must have sealed Sir Richard Blunt's delight that day. He had arrested a mass-murderer, probably the worst ever known in London, and he had the evidence of Todd's partner to help convict him. The magistrate left behind two of his officers at 186 Fleet Street with orders to comb every inch of the property and list each item they found. The pair were to have their work cut out during the new few days, so enormous did the tasks prove.

The news of Mrs Lovett's arrest had spread through London like wildfire. But the horror which had greeted the revelations about what had been going on in her shop was far surpassed on the following day by the announcement from the Bow Street Office in Craven Street that Sweeney Todd had been arrested for murder and suspected collusion with the pie-maker of Bell Yard.

London had never known such a sensation before. What little information the newspapers were supplied with before the trial was more than compensated for by public rumour, as an undated clipping from *The Examiner* of this time makes plain:

'By the time the police office at Bow Street had opened the following morning, a wild, vague and uncertain rumour had spread itself over London concerning the discoveries that had been made at Sweeney Todd's house in Fleet Street and Mrs Lovett's in Bell Yard, Temple Bar.

'The affair lost nothing from many tongued rumour and the popular belief was that Sweeney Todd's house had been found full of dead bodies from the attics to the cellars, while Mrs Lovett had been actually detected in the very act of scraping some dead man's bones for tit-bits to make a veal pie.

'Dense crowds assembled in Fleet Street to have a look at Todd's new shut-up house, and that thoroughfare, in consequence, very soon became no thoroughfare at all. Bell Yard, too, was so completely blocked up that the lawyers who were in the habit of using it as a short cut from the Temple to Lincoln's Inn were forced to take a diversion through Chancery Lane instead.

'In Bow Street, and round the doors of the police office there, was a dense crowd, too, anxious for news of the affair, and it was only with the greatest difficulty that the officers and others connected with the police inquiries could get in and out as occasion required.'

Interest in the case was to continue unabated in the weeks which followed, while Sir Richard Blunt busied himself preparing the evidence for the trial. He was to wish things could have moved faster when, a few days before Christmas, he received a crushing piece of information from Newgate. Mrs Lovett had somehow managed to get hold of some poison and had been found dead in her cell.

The details have never been quite clear as to just how the widow managed to obtain the poison with which she committed suicide. Probably because she was a woman of means she was able to pay one of the guards to have some clean clothes from home brought in to her; and it is possible there was a vial of poison concealed in one of the dresses in readiness for such an eventuality.

In any event, her body was discovered at about eight o'clock one morning just before Christmas. And with her death the prosecution lost one of their best witnesses against Sweeney Todd, for she had, since her arrest, once again confirmed to Sir

Richard Blunt that she was prepared to turn King's Evidence. Now there would be no answer to perhaps the most intriguing question of all: *why* did she agree to help Sweeney Todd in concealing his monstrous crimes? In her confession she said nothing beyond being his 'willing' accomplice. But was she willing because of her love for Todd? Or because she was afraid of him?

The news of Mrs Lovett's death dismayed Sir Richard Blunt who immediately ordered an inquiry into what had occurred. He also gave instructions that Sweeney Todd was not to be told about her death and the guard on him was to be redoubled. He did not want to lose the barber, too, especially with his trial only days away.

Christmas in London that year of 1801 was almost completely overshadowed by the coming trial of the 'Demon Barber of Fleet Street', as he had become known in the public prints. A leading article in the *Daily Courant* stated:

'Scarcely ever in London has such an amount of public excitement been produced by any criminal proceedings as by the trial of Sweeney Todd. The most hideous crimes have been laid to his charge, and, in the imagination of the people, the number of his victims has been quadrupled.

'So great is the excitement that sober-minded men, who do not see any peculiar interest in the sayings and doings of a great criminal, are disgusted that the popular taste should run that way. Be that as it may, the case of Rex v. Sweeney Todd will certainly be one of the trials of the age.'

And so it proved to be, as the account later prepared by *The Newgate Calendar*, from which I propose to quote at length, indicates. Such were the numbers of people trying to get into the Old Bailey for the trial, it says, that extra guards had to be placed in the court. The prisoner himself was brought from Newgate in irons which secured his ankles and wrists together and only enabled him to shuffle forward a few inches at a time.

It was only just before his departure for the court that Todd had been told of the death of Mrs Lovett. He looked, thereafter, the report says, 'like some great, gaunt ghost'. The haranguing he received from the sea of faces on all sides as he was lead into the court for the proceedings to begin could not have helped his complexion, either.

Once order had been restored in the packed Old Bailey, the judge and jury were told that the prisoner was charged with the murder of one Francis Thornhill, and he had originally been indicted with a female named Lovett. She, though, had taken her own life while in custody. The Attorney-General, who was presenting the prosecution's case, then began his address.

'The prisoner at the bar has been in business as a barber in Fleet Street for some years,' he said. 'Where he has continued to reside until his arrest upon the serious charge which we are brought here to investigate. What were the pursuits of the prisoner during his occupancy of that house, it is not our province just now to enquire, as all our attention must be directed to the consideration of the one charge, to which he stands at the bar of this court.'

The lawyer then began to outline the evidence that Sir Richard Blunt and his men had so painstakingly gathered from their investigations into the contents of Sweeney Todd's shop and the vaults of St Dunstan's Church.

'It appears that upon the third day of August last, a ship of 400 tons burthen, called *The Star*, arrived in the London Docks. On board that ship was the captain, a crew of nine seamen, and two boys. As passengers there were a Colonel Jeffrey and the Mr Thornhill whose death is the motive of these preceedings.

'Now this Mr Thornhill had been commissioned to take a certain string of Oriental pearls, valued at about £16,000, to a young lady in London. He was anxious to fulfil this request, and as soon as the ship docked went into the City with the pearls. It appears that upon his route to deliver them, he went into the shop of the prisoner at the bar to be shaved, and no one ever saw him come out again.'

The Attorney-General hitched his gown around his shoulders and went on without a pause: 'My Lord and gentlemen of the jury, when Mr Thornhill did not return, the captain of the ship and Colonel Jeffrey became very anxious about him and made every inquiry as to his whereabouts. They questioned the prisoner at the bar, who admitted that he had shaved Mr Thornhill, but he had left the shop when the operation was over.

'When *The Star* and her captain were forced to leave London for Bristol,' the Attorney General continued, 'Colonel Jeffrey decided to remain in the City to continue his inquiries as he felt sure that such a valuable string of pearls was bound to turn up again.

'Gentlemen, it did,' he said. 'It appeared at the Hammersmith residence of Mr John Mundel who lent money upon securities, and it will be deposed that one evening the prisoner at the bar went to this Mr Mundell and pawned a string of pearls for £1,000. It is to be regretted that this Mundell cannot be brought before the jury for he is dead. But a confidential clerk, who saw the prisoner at the bar, will depose the facts.' The Attorney General paused. 'These facts,' he went on, 'connect the prisoner with the disappearance of Thornhill — but now we come to the strongest features of this remarkable case. It appears that for a considerable time the Church of St Dunstan's in Fleet Street had become insufferable from a peculiar stench which seemed to fill the entire edifice, and quite baffled the authorities.'

The Attorney General explained to the court that no one had thought to thoroughly examine the vaults until Sir Richard Blunt, the police-magistrate, had undertaken the task. 'Gentlemen of the jury,' he said, 'Sir Richard found that almost every vault was full of the fresh remains of the dead. He found that into old coffins, the tenants of which had mouldered to dust, there had been thrust fresh bodies, with scarcely any flesh remaining on them — but yet sufficient to produce the stench in the church. One vault was found, the contents of which are too horrid to describe, but suffice to say that it contained what butchers when speaking of slaughtered animals call "offal".'

Even the hardened people of London well used to hearing ghastly tales of atrocities fell silent at this. All their eyes were on the Attorney-General as he continued with his remarks:

'Well, my Lord and gentlemen of the jury, Sir Richard persevered in his investigations and found that there was an underground connection from beneath the shaving shop of the prisoner, and the cellarage of a house in Bell Yard, Temple Bar, which was occupied by a female named Lovett, who this day should have stood at the bar beside the prisoner had she not, despite every vigilance used to prevent such an act, succeeded in poisoning herself while in prison in Newgate.

'It will be shown in evidence that the way the larger portion of the flesh of Sweeney Todd's victims was got rid of was by converting it into meat and pork-pies on the premises of Mrs Lovett.'

Even though what the prosecuting counsel had said was common gossip around London, his words still drew an audible gasp from the packed public benches. When silence had fallen once again, the Attorney-General went on to describe Sweeney Todd's revolving chair in which he had killed his victims or left them so stunned that he could easily cut their throats.

'And now, my Lord, and you gentlemen of the jury, may ask what these wholesale murders have to do with the indictment which simply charges the prisoner with the wilful murder of Francis Thornhill? To this I reply that it is impossible to make apparent to the court the method by which Francis Thornhill came to his death without going into these painful details.'

The Attorney-General paused once more and then delivered a second bombshell into the quiet of the packed Old Bailey courtroom.

'Sweeney Todd's house was found crammed with property and clothing sufficient for *160 people*.'

For a moment there was a stunned silence. Men and women looked at each other in disbelief. Had they heard right? The rumours had suggested he might have cut the throats of *dozens* of victims. But *over a hundred*! Could it possibly be true?

'Yes, gentlemen of the jury,' the barrister spoke with heavy emphasis in his voice as if to dispel any doubts, 'I said 160 people, and among all that clothing was found a piece of jacket which will be sworn to have belonged to Francis Thornhill.'

In repeating that number, *The Newgate Calendar* reported, the counsel released 'a thrill of horror' into the court, and it was to be some moments before order could be restored and the proceedings continue.

'But, my Lord, is a piece of sleeve enough to convict a man? Wisely, the law says no and looks for the body of a murdered man. Indeed, I do not call to mind an instance of a conviction where there has not been some satisfactory identification of the remains of the murdered man. We will produce that proof.

'For among the skeletons found contiguous to Todd's premises was one which will be sworn to as being that of the deceased Mr Thornhill. One bone of that skeleton will be produced in court and sworn to by a surgeon, Doctor Steers, who had the care of it and who, from repeated examinations such as only he could make, knows it well. That, my Lord and gentlemen of the jury, is all I have to say for the prosecution.'

As the Attorney-General sat down, all eyes in the courtroom turned upon Sweeney Todd. He had sat impassively throughout the address and still nothing seemed to disturb his features even now.

The first witness was Arthur Rose Ford, the captain of *The Star*, who confirmed that Francis Thornhill had sailed on his ship, been in possession of a string of valuable pearls, and had never been seen again after his visit to Sweeney Todd's shop. Into the witness box after him came Colonel William Jeffrey who also gave his account of the disappearance of Francis Thornhill, and how he had gone to Sir Richard Blunt to ask for his help.

'I accompanied Sir Richard and Doctor Steers to Sweeney Todd's shop,' the Colonel said, 'and in the vaults below, saw the Doctor take a bone from there. I made a mark on the bone to ensure its identification.'

The smartly dressed military man had hardly stepped down from the witness box, than his place was filled by the tall and impressive figure of Sir Richard Blunt. His was the evidence that all London had been waiting to hear. This was the Bow Street Runner who had run the cut-throat killer to ground. For the first time, too, Sweeney Todd was observed to look up at the man in the box. He was even noticed to cup a hand to one of his ears as if to hear better.

The police-magistrate was asked by the Attorney-General to relate in his own words his part in the events now before the court. In a quiet and precise voice, Sir Richard started by explaining how his attention had been drawn to the number of people who had unaccountably disappeared in the vicinity of Fleet Street.

'Not a trace could be found of many respectable men who had left their homes upon various objects and never returned to them,' Sir Richard said. 'The most striking peculiarity of this affair was that the men who disappeared were for the most part substantial citizens who were far from likely to have yielded to any of those temptations that at times bring the young and heedless in this city into fearful dangers. I saw the Secretary of State upon the matter and it was agreed that I was to have *carte blanche* to give my time and attention to unravelling the mystery.

'After careful inquiry, I found that out of thirteen disappearances, no less than ten had declared their intention to get shaved, or their hair dressed, or to go through some process which required them to visit a barber. I then personally called at all the barbers' shops in the neighbourhood — but never alone.

'The fact that I had someone waiting for me in the shop doubtless saved my life — for *I* was several times shaved and dressed by the prisoner at the bar.'

Sir Richard's words resounded in the stillness of the Old Bailey with all the impact of the earlier surprises which the case had produced. One legend suggests that Sweeney Todd himself sat bolt upright in his chair at this confession by the Bow Street Runner. The very man who was now the main witness against him could so easily have been numbered among his victims.

The magistrate admitted to the court that he had found nothing suspicious on any of these visits, though he remembered that on a couple of occasions the barber had attempted to get Sir Richard's companion to leave the shop on some pretext. When the man had refused to go, Sweeney Todd had 'gone on with the shaving in the coolest possible manner'.

The breakthrough in his investigations had come with the reports of the strange smell at St Dunstan's, Sir Richard told the court.

'My attention was directed to the peculiar odour in the church and from that moment I, in my own mind, connected it with Sweeney Todd and the disappearances of the persons who had so unaccountably been lost in the immediate neighbourhood of Fleet Street. And in the midst of this, I had a formal application made to me concerning the disappearance of Mr Francis Thornhill, who had been clearly traced to the shop of the prisoner at the bar and never seen by anyone to leave it.'

Convinced, now, that the solution to the mystery lay in or below Sweeney Todd's shop, the magistrate said he had instituted a thorough search unknown to the owner.

'In the cellar beneath the shop, the first object that presented itself to me was a chair fixed to the roof by its legs. The chair I at once recognised as identical to the one in the shop in which I had sat. In a moment the whole truth burst upon me.'

Following his discovery of this chair which precipitated the unsuspecting victims into the cellar, Sir Richard said he next found some bodies hidden in the vaults and then the passageway to Mrs Lovett's pie shop in Bell Yard.

'Prosecuting my researches, I also found that no meat from any butcher or salesman ever found its way to the pie shop,' he continued. 'The supply of flesh was human and that was the way the prisoner had got rid of the greater part of his victims.

'Measures were then taken to prevent any more murders by persons in my force always following anyone into the barber's shop. Then, when the evidence was all ready by the finding and identifying of Mr Francis Thornhill's leg-bone, I took measures to apprehend the prisoner.'

One final witness for the prosecution then entered the box, Doctor Sylvester Steers, the specialist who had identified the leg bone of the murder victim.

The Doctor told the court of his visit to the vaults of St Dunstan's Church.

'I found there a great quantity of osteological remains, human bones,' he said, 'and among them a male femur, or thigh bone, which I have with me.'

As Doctor Steers spoke, *The Newgate Calendar* reports, he took from the pocket of his great-coat, a small packet wrapped in brown paper. Untying some string, he extracted a small bone and handed it to a court official. 'It was passed to the jury,' says the report, 'but several shrank from it.'

The Attorney-General addressed the witness: 'Can you, sir, on your oath and without the slightest reservation, tell my Lord and the gentlemen of the jury, whose thigh bone this is?'

'I can. It is the thigh bone of Mr Francis Thornhill.'

'Will you tell the court the grounds upon which you arrived at that conclusion?'

'Certainly. Mr Thornhill met with a very unusual and painful accident. The external condyle or projection on the outer end of the thigh bone, which makes part of the knee-joint, was broken off, and there was a diagonal fracture about three inches higher up upon the bone. I had the sole care of the case, and although a cure was effected, it was not without considerable distortion of the bone and general disarrangement of the adjacent parts.'

Doctor Steers added, 'From my frequent examination I was perfectly well acquainted with the case, and I can swear that the bone in the hands of the jury was the one so broken and to which I attended.'

The Attorney-General had one final question for the witness. 'Did you ever have a similar case to that of Mr Thornhill's under your treatment?'

'No, sir. Never a precisely similar one.'

As the Doctor climbed down from the witness box and returned to his seat, the bone which he had brought as evidence was retrieved by the court official from the last of the jurors and placed carefully on the table in front of the legal counsels. There was undeniably something both eloquent and unnerving about that mute object which, for a moment in time, held the attention of every person in the packed courtroom of the Old Bailey. Could something so insignificant from such an overwhelming horror finally bring the terrible Demon Barber of Fleet Street to justice?

12

'Foul and Unnatural Murder'

The Newgate Calendar, in describing the trial of Sweeney Todd, states that it was 'quite clear to even the most superficial observer that the murder of Francis Thornhill had been just picked out for convenience sake, and was one among many'. When the counsel who had been appointed to represent the barber stood up to begin his defence, it was also soon apparent he was bent upon ridiculing the evidence that had been presented concerning the human bone which lay on the table in front of him.

'May it please your Lordship and gentlemen of the jury,' he began, 'I have, upon the part of my client, most seriously to complain about the vast amount of extraneous matter that has been mixed up with this case. To one grain of wheat we have had whole bunches of chaff, and gentlemen have been brought here surely to amuse the court with long-winded romances.

'My client is clearly and distinctly charged with the murder of one Francis Thornhill, and, instead of any evidence, near or remote fixing the deed upon him, we have nothing but long stories about vaults, bad odours in churches, movable floor-boards, chairs standing on their heads, secret passages and pork pies. Really, gentlemen of the jury, I do think that the manner in which the prosecution has been got up against my virtuous and pious client is an outrage to your common sense.'

On hearing these words, an undercurrent of laughter arose from the public benches and the judge banged his gavel sharply several times to restore order. The defending counsel continued, totally unperturbed.

'This is nothing but the attempt to take the life of a man from a variety of circumstances external to the real charge to which he is called upon here to plead. Let us examine the sort of evidence upon which it had been thought proper to put a fellow creature to this bar upon a charge affecting his life.'

The speaker was clearly warming to his task and wondered, first, what the fact that a number of respectable men leaving their homes and never returning had to do with the death of Francis Thornhill?

'Then we are told that the respectable men want to get shaved,' he said. 'And that Sir Richard Blunt had a shave several times at my client's shop, yet here he is quite alive and well to give evidence today, and no one will say that Sir Richard is not a respectable man.'

The barrister paused as if to let his words sink in. He shuffled the sheaves of paper on the table in front of him before going on.

'Next we have the bad smell in the Church of St Dunstan. Really, gentlemen of the jury, you might well say that my client committed felony because this court was not well ventilated!'

For the second time that morning, a little wave of laughter broke the stillness of the Old Bailey. When it had subsided, defence counsel returned to his attack on the assumption that because Francis Thornhill had not been seen to come out of Sweeney Todd's shop he must have been murdered there.

'Really,' the barrister protested, 'this is too bad. Hundreds of people may have seen him come out — and no doubt did so — but they happened not to know him. So just because no one passed the time of day with this man, my client is declared guilty of murder.'

Pausing once again, the lawyer lent forward and lifted up the piece of bone from the table in front of him.

'Then we are told about this bone, and that it is declared to be the bone of the deceased. Gentlemen of the jury, what would you think of a man who should produce a brick and swear that it belonged to a certain house?

'I do think that you will soon see upon what a string of sophistry the evidence against my client rests. Who shall take it upon himself to say that Mr Thornhill is not alive and well somewhere? We all know that persons connected with the sea are rather uncertain in their movements.'

Shuffling his papers once again, the defence lawyer then turned on his heels to indicate the prisoner in the dock.

'My client, your Lordship and gentlemen of the jury, has a plain, unvarnished tale to tell which will clear him from any suspicions,' he said. 'Mr Todd is a religious man, as anyone may see by the mild and gentlemanly look of his amiable countenance. He took the premises in Fleet Street in the pursuit of his most useful calling and he had no more idea that there was a movable floor in his shop, and that his shaving chair would go down with anyone, than an unborn child.

'Is it really likely that a man who could stoop to such baseness as to make money by murder would occupy himself with such a trivial employment as shaving for a penny? The deceased gentleman, Mr Francis Thornhill — if he be deceased at all — came into my worthy client's shop to be shaved, and was at that time a little the worse for drink that he had indulged himself with, no doubt, as he came along.

'My client did indeed shave him and he said that he had to go along and see a young lady. When he was shaved, Mr Thornhill left and went towards Fleet market. My client watched him from his door and actually saw him get into an argument with a porter at the top of the market. Then as another person came in to be shaved, my client returned into his shop and saw no more of Mr Thornhill.'

Referring to Todd as a 'man well-known for his benevolence and piety in Fleet Street', the barrister said that even during the time when the appalling smell at St Dunstan's was keeping many parishioners away, he faithfully attended the services: 'I ask you as men, my Lord and gentlemen of the jury, if you could do that in the knowledge that you had committed a murder?'

In his closing remarks, the defence counsel turned to the story of Mrs Lovett.

'My Lord, it is for my client a most unfortunate thing that a person named Lovett, who kept a pie shop in Bell Yard, is not now in the land of the living. If she were so, there is no doubt that she would have told some true tale of how the vaults beneath the old church connected with her shop, and so cleared the prisoner at the bar of all participation in her crimes.

'That murder has been committed in conjunction with that woman, who committed suicide, rather than come forward and clear my client, against whom she had a spite, there can be no doubt.

'Gentlemen of the jury, it is the wrong man who now stands at the bar. The real murderer has yet to be discovered. I therefore call upon you in the name of justice to acquit my client.'

There can be little doubt that this lawyer faced with the unenviable task of defending Sweeney Todd gave a bravura performance, if a little theatrical and overstated. When asked by the judge if he proposed to call any witnesses, the defence counsel replied, 'No, no. Innocence is its own best safeguard.'

According to *The Newgate Calendar*, the Attorney-General then waived his right of reply. The judge's summing up was brief and to the point.

'The sequence of evidence by which it is attempted to bring this crime home to the prisoner at the bar lies within a very small compass indeed,' he said, 'Firstly, there is the tracing of Francis Thornhill to the prisoner's shop and his disappearance from thence. Then there is the thigh bone sworn to be that of Francis Thornhill and certainly found in such contiguity to his premises as to warrant a belief that he placed it there. Gentlemen of the jury, the case is in your hands.'

According to most accounts, the jury debated for less than five minutes before delivering their verdict: 'Guilty.'

Pandemonium broke out among the spectators and it was some time before the judge could again restore order. Then, says *The Newgate Calendar*, 'All eyes were turned upon the most dastardly criminal of the age, Sweeney Todd, who stood in the dock glaring at the foreman of the jury.'

The sentencing of criminals in 1802 did not require the judge to withdraw first. He simply took up a black cap and placed it over his wig.

'Prisoner at the bar,' he said, 'you stand convicted after a most patient trial by an impartial jury of your fellow countrymen, and on the clearest evidence, of the foul and unnatural murder of Francis Thornhill. It was a cold-blooded, dastardly deed. You must therefore prepare to leave this world and make your peace in another.

'On me only rests the painful duty of passing the dread sentence of the law. Have you anything to say why that sentence, which is one of death, should not be passed upon you?'

Sweeney Todd's response to this invitation are, apparently, almost as many and varied as the subsequent versions of his life and crimes. It has been suggested he immediately pleaded insanity; that he claimed he was the victim of a conspiracy; and that if Mrs Lovett had been present she would have been able to prove his innocence. All that seems certain is that he shouted out, 'I am not guilty!'

Before passing sentence the judge addressed a few further remarks concerning Sweeney Todd's crimes which would certainly be considered inappropriate today — if not actually ruled inadmissable — but which undoubtedly helped cement the legend of the Demon Barber.

'Sweeney Todd,' he said, 'you have been convicted of the crime of murder, and certain circumstances which it would have been improper to produce before this court in the progress of your trial, lead irresistibly to the belief that your life for years past has been one frightful scene of murder. Not only the unhappy gentleman for whose murder you now stand here has suffered from your frightful practices, but many others.

'It will be a satisfaction, too, to the court and the jury to know that the woman named Lovett, who the prisoner said would and could prove his innocence had she been alive, made, shortly before her death, a full confession, wherein she inculpated you most fearfully.'

The judge paused, cleared his throat and added, 'It is now my painful duty to pass upon you the sentence of the law, which is that you be taken from here to a place of execution and hanged by the neck until dead. May Heaven have mercy upon you. You cannot expect that society can do otherwise than put out of life someone who, like yourself, has been a terror and a scourge.'

The judge stood up and the court rose with him. Before Todd could protest any further he was hurried out of the courtroom as fast as the iron shackles on his legs would allow, and back to Newgate.

* * *

The legend of the Demon Barber was reported for all to read in the following days and weeks in the pages of newspapers and pamphlets. A thriving trade was also done in a 'most exact likeness of Sweeney Todd the Murderer, drawn from life while he was on trial,' according to the hawkers who peddled them at three pence a copy. (A rare example which has survived is reproduced in this book. The man who had made corpses into meat pies also quickly became a bogeyman for parents to use to frighten naughty children. Conversely, the barbers of London found themselves being looked at with suspicion for months after the trial, and the trade in meat pasties suffered disastrously, too.

Not surprisingly, a favourite topic of gossip in the streets and taverns of London concerned just how many victims Sweeney Todd might have dispatched. A gaoler in Newgate Prison who claimed to have had charge of Todd, said that the barber had awoken from a nightmare one morning and told him he had been haunted all night long by the faces of his victims, 'a sailor, a quaker, a hundred others'. Other than this rather circumstantial story, the truth is that Todd never himself disclosed any figure.

Although evidence of all the clothing found in Sweeney Todd's shop adds weight to the figure of 'over 160 victims' quoted in court, it was not until 1831 that more remains found in the vaults beneath St Dunstan's Church went some way towards confirming it. A group of workmen engaged on rebuilding the church, dug up several heaps of bones all along an underground passageway stretching from Fleet Street to Chancery Lane. This had apparently been the route taken by Todd on his journeys to Mrs Lovett's pie-shop, and the bones were believed to be those of earlier victims he had buried before resorting to using the vaults which Sir Richard Blunt had stumbled upon. Even this, however, may not have been the full total, for the evidence suggests his reign of terror extended for almost seventeen years, and that he may well, at the height of his crimes, have been 'polishing off' a victim every month. We shall never know.

It is true that after his execution the facts about Sweeney Todd rapidly became distorted. Indeed, in most subsequent accounts of his life it is maintained that he was hung in Tyburn, the favourite spot for dispatching highwaymen. This, however, is patently untrue. Although Tyburn, which stood on a spot now occupied by the famous London landmark, Marble Arch, had been the place of execution for criminals since the twelfth century, records clearly state that it ceased this function in 1783 after the completion of the new Newgate Prison.

'Thereafter,' says Peter Aykroyd in his study of *Evil London* (1973), 'all criminals convicted of capital crimes committed in the city of London or the County of Middlesex were hanged there. There were pertinent reasons for the transfer of the function. The processions to Tyburn had become an "obstacle to traffic and a hindrance to business". Also, residents in the Tyburn neighbourhood which had become fashionable not only disliked the mobs which assembled for the executions but also disapproved of the gallows being so close to their houses.'

So much, I am afraid, for all the colourful tales of Sweeney Todd being transported in an open cart through the city of London in front of huge, jeering crowds, to be strung up at Tyburn. To the readers of the first 'penny dreadfuls', a death in the tradition of the 'knights of the road' was doubtless much more in keeping with Todd's grisly reputation than an execution in front of the grey walls of Newgate Prison. Indeed, it is not difficult to understand how the authors of this cheap form of literature found it much more satisfying to write, 'Those who found themselves unwitting cannibals through Sweeney Todd pelted him all the way to the gallows.'

What is a fact is that Sweeney Todd was taken from his cell in Newgate Prison at 8 a.m. on the morning of Tuesday, 25 January, 1802 and hung on a portable scaffold erected near the

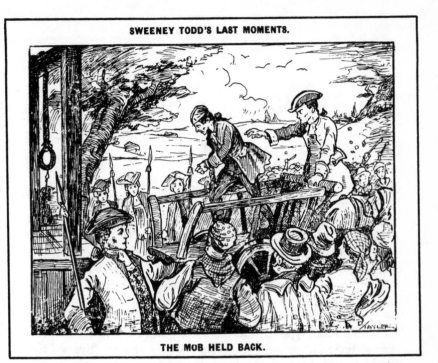

SWEENEY TODD'S LAST MOMENTS.

THE MOB HELD BACK.

Huge crowds gathered to watch the execution of Sweeney Todd on January 25, 1802.

main gate in front of a crowd estimated at many thousands. He apparently 'died hard' on the gallows, but there is no record of any last minute confession or admission.

Thereafter, as was customary, Todd's body was taken down after hanging for an hour and removed to the Royal College of Surgeons in the Old Bailey for dissection. This fate was considered part of any sentence for murder. It seemed doubly appropriate, too, to all those who had followed the course of the Demon Barber's crimes, that he should end his days as a pile of flesh, bones and offal.

The greatest mass murderer in British history was just forty-six years old.

13

The Making of a Legend

It was not until forty-five years after the horrific events that I have described took place that the name of Sweeney Todd again appeared in print. This time it was in the pages of a weekly newspaper, *The People's Periodical and Family Library*, and it was from that moment that the legend about the Demon Barber, which still excites such interest today, really began to develop.

The People's Periodical was a sixteen-page paper about the same size as a modern women's magazine, illustrated with an engraving on the front page, and set in three columns of extremely small type. It featured mostly stories of romance with essays, reviews, answers to reader's letters and an 'Every-Day Book' of useful facts and figures. Material was obviously drawn from far and wide, and short stories by famous contemporary authors such as Charles Dickens and Edgar Allan Poe appeared frequently — doubtless reprinted without permission or payment because copyright protection of writers' work was then virtually non-existent. Although *The People's Periodical* serialised a few stories that enjoyed a certain popularity such as *Rose Somerville*, *Grace Weldon* and *The Fated Lovers of Bourdon*, it was the Sweeney Todd tale that has earned it a place in publishing history.

Copies of this publication are today fabulously rare — neither the British Museum nor the Bodlian Library possess any at all — and some writers have even suggested that, like the existence of the Demon Barber, it might even be wholly fictitious. I have, however, been able to trace a complete run of the publication which belongs to a collector of 'penny dreadfuls', David Philips, and, thanks to his kindness I can confirm not only its existence, but also that within its pages resides the very first novelisation to feature Sweeney Todd. It is certainly a seminal work in the legend of the Demon Barber.

Todd made his bow in issue number seven of *The People's Periodical*, dated 21 November, 1846, as a character in a serial with the quite unremarkable title of *The String of Pearls: A Romance*. No author was credited for the story which began on the front page, although underneath the journal's masthead were the words, 'Edited by E. Lloyd'. Lloyd was also credited on the back page as being the printer and publisher, at his offices, 12 Salisbury Square, Fleet Street — a singularly appropriate address, I could not help thinking as I turned the fragile pages.

There was no hint, initially, that *The String of Pearls* was anything other than one of the magazine's usual pieces of romantic fiction; certainly nothing to suggest that it would feature real people and real events. Research has subsequently shown that this was an element frequently to be found in Lloyd's publications: he and his writers borrowed as freely from life as they did from fiction!

Although Sweeney Todd is introduced to the readers in the opening pages of the story, the half page engraving which accompanied the first episode depicted one of the most traditional situations in romantic literature — a pretty, tearful young girl, the heroine, Johanna Oakley, being comforted by her father. It was hardly the most dramatic introduction for a story that would run to thirty-seven chapters in eighteen subsequent issues, and help transform a sordid London murderer into a world-famous character. I shall return to the story and its plot shortly, but it is also interesting to discover something about the man who published the serial and the now virtually-forgotten writer who gave the Fleet Street Barber a fictional life all of his own.

Edward Lloyd (1815–1890) who described himself as the Editor of *The People's Periodical*, has subsequently become known as the founder of the 'Salisbury Square School of Fiction' — named after his address — and was certainly the most famous publisher of those weekly serials of the Victorian era known as 'Penny Bloods' or 'Penny Dreadfuls'. Although he made a fortune from these highly ephemeral publications, he later turned his back on such material and thereafter became a general newspaper publisher of — among other titles — *The Penny Sunday Times*, which later became *Lloyd's Weekly News* and survived well into the middle of the twentieth century as *The Sunday News*.

Lloyd, the son of a Thornton Heath farmer, was one of the pioneers of cheap literature for the masses in England. He took advantage of innovations in the printing industry, such as the development of the rotary steam printing press and the creation of paper-making machines, and the introduction of basic education for everyone, all of which were occurring at the onset of the nineteenth century, to do so. He himself had little formal education, but when he opened a small shop in London to sell books, newspapers and comic valentines, he quickly sensed a need for cheap, printed reading matter at a time when most literature was being published in expensive two and three volume books.

Working in London, Lloyd also became aware of the public's fascination with crime and criminals, and his very first publications in the late 1830s, sold for a penny and embellished with 'fierce' engravings, were full of such characters as their titles bear witness: *Lives of the Most Notorious Highwaymen*, *The History of Pirates* and *The Calendar of Horrors* (an unashamed plagiarism of *The Newgate Calendar*).

The stories were scarcely works of literature. Most were churned out by poorly paid hacks who were encouraged to steal mercilessly from any sources and 'beef up' the material if the facts were not exciting or gruesome enough for a predominantly working-class market. Indeed, Lloyd and his successors often demonstrated their indifference to any finer feelings their readers might have by abruptly discontinuing episodes of the stories on one page of an issue, and then continuing in the next without even a word of 'what had gone before'!

With the benefit of hindsight, there can be little doubt that the engravings which adorned these 'penny dreadfuls' played an important part in their success, and it was by no means uncommon for a publication whose sales were flagging to have a sensational and even totally irrelevant picture inserted in an attempt to bolster public interest. If this had no effect, the whole story might well be brought to a speedy conclusion in the next issue without the least regard to the complexity of plot or variety of characters and the different situations in which they were involved.

In the twenty years between 1836 and 1856, Edward Lloyd published well over 200 such 'bloods' on almost every imaginable subject, but of all these, only two are remembered today: *The String of Pearls* which featured Sweeney Todd, and *Varney the Vampire*, a mammoth serial of 220 chapters about a marauding vampire in England which was published in penny parts in 1847. Both of these stories are credited to a single member of Lloyd's team of writers, a remarkable man by the name of Thomas Peckett Prest.

Prest is one of the most intriguing figures in the whole field of mass market literature. Historian W. O. G. Lofts, who has researched Prest's life, says that a very old man he spoke to some years back who had a personal knowledge of the writer described him as a 'morbid genius' who was regarded by his readers at the time as something of a second Edgar Allan Poe. However inflated such a claim may be, Mr Lofts is right in stating that Prest deserves better than to be totally ignored by all biographical dictionaries, for he was a writer of prodigious output and variety, and was certainly the most important of Lloyd's contributors. Despite the difficulty in attribution because of the lack of author credit on most of the Lloyd publications, Prest more than likely wrote over half of the 'penny bloods' originating from Salisbury Square.

According to the available evidence, Prest was born about 1810 into a comparatively affluent London family. He appears to have developed an absorbing passion for writing during his childhood — as well as a taste for languages, music and drama — and first ventured into print with some essays, articles and short stories contributed to weekly magazines in the 1830s. In November 1835 he took his first major step in journalism when he was appointed editor of *The Magazine of Curiosity and Wonder*, published by G. Drake of Clare Market, London, a publication packed with items about the strange and the mysterious. Despite its obvious appeal, the magazine only lasted for twenty-nine issues, but it undoubtedly furthered Prest's fascination with the bizarre.

His interest in music and the theatre saw him for a time act as editor of *The London Singer's Magazine*, as well as composing a number of music hall songs for popular artists of the day like George Leybourne, 'The Great Vance'. Prest continued to develop his connections with the stage, and he later adapted a number of farces and melodramas from the French. He was also for a time associated with the Britannia Theatre in Hoxton, and between 1841 and 1849 wrote several plays for the manager, Sam Lane. We shall be returning to this association later when discussing the history of Sweeney Todd in the theatre.

But undoubtedly the association which kept him busiest was the one with Edward Lloyd whom he met around 1840. By all accounts, Prest was already displaying some of the unstable elements in his character, drinking heavily and always in debt. Lloyd, who could offer him immediate payment on delivery of each episode of a serial, was just the sort of man the improvident Prest would be attracted to, and there are stories that at the peak of his production he was turning in episodes for as many as six serials per week. For this he would be paid ten shillings per episode. The fact he was so busy for Lloyd seems to dispel another story that he was unreliable — although there does not seem much doubt that he regularly changed his address to avoid his creditors.

It should be no surprise to learn that the pressures of all this work, plus his heavy drinking, damaged Prest's health: he died in 1859, aged forty-nine. He had apparently been consumptive for years, and it seems a cruel trick of fate that while Lloyd who had published his work prospered and made a fortune, Prest died penniless. He had, though, ensured a little piece of fame for himself with his version of the Sweeney Todd story in *The String of Pearls*. Quite where he came across the details or why he decided to submerge the grisly Demon Barber in a love story (other than to spare the stomachs of the more delicate readers of *The People's Periodical*!) is not known. It has even been suggested that Prest actually invented the character from a composite of names and the earlier stories of Sawney Beane and the cut-throat Parisian barber in the Rue des Marmouzets. My conviction is much simpler: Prest used *The Newgate Calendar* (which Lloyd had, of course, earlier plagiarised) as his sole source of reference. And to these facts he added his imagination and some new characters.

What is, though, beyond doubt is that Thomas Peckett Prest's novelisation was to inspire the later versions of the story which have ensured Sweeney Todd's immortality — like him or loath him. And for that Prest deserves the credit which has so long been denied.

* * *

Prest's story of *The String of Pearls* is set in Fleet Street in the year 1785. Prest's characterisation of Sweeney Todd is, however, rather less of a terrifying figure than the real-life 'Demon Barber'.

'The barber was a long, low-jointed, ill-put-together sort of fellow,' the first episode informed readers. 'He has an immense mouth, and such huge hands and feet that he was, in his way, quite a natural curiosity. What was more wonderful, considering his trade, was that there never was such a head of hair as Sweeney Todd's. It was a most terrific head of hair, and as the barber kept all his combs in it — some people said his scissors likewise — when he put his head out of the shop door to see what sort of weather it was, he might be mistaken for some Indian warrior with a very remarkable head-dress.'

Todd is also said to have a squint and 'a disagreeable kind of unmirthful laugh which came at all sorts of odd times and would sometimes make people start, especially when they were being shaved'.

In short, though, the author said, 'People thought him a careless enough, harmless fellow, with not much sense in him, and at times they almost considered he was a little cracked. But there were others, again, who shook their heads when they spoke of him, and while they could say nothing to his prejudice, except that they certainly considered he was odd. But for all that, he did a most thriving business; and was considered by his neighbours to be a very well-to-do sort of man, and decidedly, in city phraseology, "warm".'

As the story opens, Todd has just taken on a new apprentice, a timid lad named Tobias Ragg, whom he has warned against spying on him or drawing conclusions from anything he sees or hears in the shop. The punishment, the boy is told, will be to have his throat cut from ear to ear.

When the barber has finished talking to Tobias a customer with a dog enters the shop. Sweeney is obviously ill-at-ease with the animal, but sends Tobias off on an errand. He then busies himself shaving the man and, in conversation, learns that his customer has just returned from a voyage to India, carrying a gift of valuable pearls for Johanna Oakley, the daughter of a local spectacle-maker, from her sweetheart, Mark Ingestre. At the mention of the pearls, Todd asks to be excused for a moment.

'Sweeney Todd walked into the back parlour and closed the door,' Thomas Prest's narrative continues. 'There was a strange sound suddenly compounded of a rushing noise and then a heavy blow, immediately after which Sweeney Todd emerged from the parlour and, folding his arms, he looked upon the vacant chair where his customer had been seated. But the customer was gone, leaving not the slightest trace of his presence behind except for his hat, and that Sweeney Todd immediately seized and thrust into a corner of the shop.'

When the customer, a Lieutenant Thornhill, fails to return to his ship, two friends set out to find him. On the way they come across the man's dog, Hector, carrying a hat in his mouth. The animal leads them unerringly back to Sweeney Todd's shop. When the barber is confronted about the missing man, he admits he had shaved him, but the man had left without his hat. The dog had later rushed in behind another customer and ran off with it, he said. Neither of the men is satisfied with Sweeney

THE
PEOPLE'S PERIODICAL
AND
FAMILY LIBRARY.

EDITED BY E. LLOYD.

No. 8. Vol. I.   FOR THE WEEK ENDING NOVEMBER 28, 1846.   [PRICE ONE PENNY.

THE STRING OF PEARLS.
A ROMANCE.

(Continued from our last.)

he captain ordered the boat to proceed up the towards the Temple stairs, where Hector's master ad expressed his intention of proceeding, and, the faithful animal saw the direction in which were going, he lay down in the bottom of the perfectly satisfied, and gave himself up to that e, of which he was evidently as much in need cannot be said that Colonel Jeffery suspected anything of a very serious nature had happened d, their principal anxiety was, when they came

considered some street grievance, and had got himself into the custody of the civil power in consequence

'Of course,' said the captain, 'Master Hector would view that as a very serious affair, and finding himself denied access to his master, you see he has come off to us, which was certainly the most prudent thing he could do, and I should not be at all surprised if he takes us to the door of some watch-house, where we shall find our friend snug enough.'

The tide was running up; and that Thornhill had not saved the turn of it, by dropping down earlier to the vessel, was one of the things that surprised the captain. However, they got up quickly, and as at that hour there was not much on the river to impede their progress, and as at that time the Thames was not a thoroughfare for little stinking steam-boats, they soon reached the ancient Temple stairs.

The dog, who had until then seemed to be asleep, suddenly sprung up, and seizing the hat again in his mouth, rushed again on shore, and was closely followed by the captain and colonel.

He led them through the Temple with great agility, pursuing with admirable tact the precise path that his master had taken towards the entrance to the Temple in Fleet-street opposite Chancery-lane.

which very much surprised those who followed him, and caused them to pause to hold a consultation ere they proceeded further. While this was proceeding Todd suddenly opened the door, and aimed a blow at the dog with an iron bar, but the latter dexterously avoided it, and, but that the door was suddenly closed again, he would have made Sweeney Todd regret such an interference.

'We must inquire into this,' said the captain; 'there seems to be mutual ill-will between that man and the dog.'

They both tried to enter the barber's shop, but it was fast on the inside; and after repeated knockings, Todd called from within, saying—

'I won't open the door while that dog is there. He is mad, or has a spite against me—I don't know nor care which—it's a fact, that's all I am aware of.'

'I will undertake,' said the captain, 'that the dog shall do you no harm; but open the door, for in we must come, and will.'

'I will take your promise,' said Sweeney Todd; 'but mind you keep it, or I shall protect myself and take the creature's life; so, if you value it, you had better hold it fast.'

The captain pacified Hector as well as he could

After his hanging, Sweeney Todd soon became a popular figure in 'penny dreadfuls'.

Todd's story, but have no evidence to contradict him. When they leave the shop, the dog insists on remaining outside the door.

The story next introduces two more important female characters. The raven-haired, blue-eyed Johanna Oakley, who is awaiting the return of her lover, Mark: and the 'buxom, young and good-looking' Mrs Lovett who keeps a famous pie shop in Bell Yard.

'Well did they deserve their reputation, her famous pies,' Prest's text says. 'There was about them a flavour never surpassed and rarely equalled. The paste was of the most delicate construction and impregnated with the aroma of a delicious gravy that defied description. Then the small portions of meat which they contained were so tender, and the fat and lean so artistically mixed up, that to eat one of Mrs Lovett's pies was such a provocative to eat another, that many persons who came to lunch stayed to dine.'

But despite all these outward signs of a prospering business, Mrs Lovett is having trouble with her pie-maker who lives and works in the cellars beneath the premises and has announced he wants to leave the job. The man seems to have discovered something unpleasant about his work. But before he can carry out his threat, he is brutally murdered by an unseen assassin. Within a day, another poor wretch in need of work who calls himself Jarvis Williams calls at the shop and is offered the post of pie-maker.

Colonel Jeffrey, one of the missing Lieutenant Thornhill's friends, has now made himself known to Johanna Oakley and tells her about the seaman's disappearance on the way to see her with the string of pearls and a message from Mark. In company with another friend, Captain Rathbone, the Colonel has also spoken to Tobias Ragg and tried to get information from him about his master's activities. The boy is too frightened to talk — and with good reason. Tobias has, in fact, already discovered the secret of the barber's revolving chair and also found a number of cupboards full of items of clothing from previous customers. When Sweeney Todd realises the boy suspects him, he wastes no time in having Tobias committed to a disreputable madhouse.

At this juncture, Johanna Oakley has come to the conclusion that only by finding out what has happened to Thornhill can she hope to learn the fate of her lover. She takes the bold decision to disguise herself as a boy and seek a job as Sweeney Todd's apprentice. Her timing proves perfect with Tobias having just been committed, and she is given the job.

Colonel Jeffrey and Captain Rathbone have also not been inactive during the interim and have taken their suspicions about Sweeney Todd to 'a reknowned city magistrate', Sir Richard Brown. He, it seems, has already been investigating some strange reports of a horrid stench emanating from St Dunstan's Church and wonders if the two facts might in some way be connected.

Events now begin to move faster in the tradition of the best 'penny dreadful' serials. First, Tobias Ragg manages to escape from the madhouse while the owner is drunk; and Johanna Oakley — now calling herself 'Charley Green' — has learned what a dangerous man Sweeney Todd can be. Just when she begins to fear for her life, however, a note is thrust into her hand by a mysterious figure who slips quickly in and out of the shop. The note is from Sir Richard Brown who tells her he has learned of her mission — 'and enterprise which, considering your youth and your sex, should have been left to others' — but in the hope that it might lead to 'unmasking the villain', she will be kept under surveillance at all times.

Sweeney Todd is also becoming increasingly nervous that his crimes may be about to catch up with him. He has obtained a large sum of money for the string of pearls and feels it might be a good opportunity to leave London. But first there is the little matter of his partner, Mrs Lovett, who, it seems, has been demanding a bigger share of the spoils. Todd pays a visit to Bell Yard and promises to share with her the money he has received from the sale of pearls.

'At this, Mrs Lovett rose and went into the shop,' the story goes on. 'The moment her back was turned, Todd produced a little bottle of poison and emptied it into the brandy decanter.

He had just succeeded in his manoeuvre, and concealed the bottle again, when she appeared and flung herself into a chair.'

Sweeney Todd returns to Fleet Street satisfied he has settled with Mrs Lovett. A man is already waiting for him in the shop and tells him he is a wealthy farmer who has just made a profitable sale. Old habits die hard, and Todd determines to 'polish off' just one more victim. He dispatches his 'apprentice' Johanna on an errand and disappears into the next room to operate the chair a last time. When Todd reappears, however, the man has sprung nimbly from the seat and is waiting there to confront him. It is none other than Sir Richard Brown. The narrative continues:

' "Murderer!" shouted Sir Richard, in a voice that rung like the blast of a trumpet through the house. In an instant he sprang upon Sweeney Todd and grappled him by the throat. There was a short struggle and they were down upon the floor together. But Todd's wrists were suddenly laid hold of, and a pair of handcuffs most scientifically put upon them by the officer who had emerged from the cupboard where he had been concealed.

' "Secure him well, my man," said the magistrate, "and don't let him lay violent hands upon himself. We have discovered the secret of the chair and they mystery of the vaults. Thank God, we have stopped his career!" '

In Mrs Lovett's shop a short while later a final batch of pies appears from the underground cellar — and with it two shocks for the owner. Firstly, a man leaps from the tray to reveal to the customers that the pies are made of human flesh. Secondly, as Mrs Lovett clutches herself in a mixture of shock and agony, she realises the brandy that she had drunk earlier to steady her nerves must have been poisoned.

Into this scene of confusion arrives a party consisting of Sir Richard Brown, Colonel Jeffrey, Tobais Ragg and Johanna Oakley, now dressed in her own clothes once more. The young girl has clearly been unhappy about visiting the shop, until the moment Sir Richard points to the sorry figure of the pie-maker. It is her missing lover, Mark Ingestre. The pair cling together in a tearful reunion.

Thomas Prest's narrative then neatly ties up the loose ends of the story. Mrs Lovett did not recover consciousness from the dose of poison that Sweeney Todd had put in her bottle, while the barber himself 'passed that night in Newgate, and in due time a swinging corpse was all that remained of the barber of Fleet Street'.

The story added, 'Beneath the old church of St Dunstan were found the heads and bones of Todd's victims. As little as possible was said by the authorities about it. But it was supposed that some hundreds of persons must have perished in the frightful manner we have detailed.'

In the best tradition of Victorian romances, Mark and Johanna were married and young Tobias taken into their service. So ended Thomas Prest's story which no doubt entertained the readers of *The People's Periodical* during the winter months of 1846–7. The author signed off his tale as simply as he had begun — and no doubt hurried round to Salisbury Square with the manuscript to collect his ten shilling fee.

'Johanna and Mark Ingestre,' he concluded, 'lived long and happily together, enjoying all the comforts of an independent existence — but they never forgot the strange and eventful circumstances connected with 'The String of Pearls'!

The couple might, indeed, have suffered the fate of so many heroes and heroines of this kind of fiction by disappearing into oblivion — except for their association with the man called Sweeney Todd. Nor could Prest himself have had the least idea as he laid down his pen for the last time of the enduring effect his 'Romance' was to have on literature and, in particular, the theatre.

14

The Barber Fiend of Melodrama

The British public's appetite for exciting entertainment in the middle years of the nineteenth century can be summed up in a single word: voracious. During the first half of the century the population had increased from eight to sixteen million, and now that an ever-growing number of these people were semi-literate and even had a little money to spare in their pockets thanks to slightly improved wages, they wanted to forget their poor living conditions and hard, repetitive work in the evenings through escapist fare of one sort or another. The development of the printing press and its product the penny journal had provided one means of satisfying this demand. The theatrical 'melodrama' — which was to draw extensively on the latter — provided the second.

The melodrama as we understand it today emerged during the last years of the eighteenth century, flourished throughout the nineteenth, and died lingeringly in the first quarter of the twentieth century. It was produced in theatres of all descriptions from the vast stages of Drury Lane and Covent Garden to the most disreputable 'penny gafs' and travelling shows. As an art form, the melodrama has too often been written off contemptuously as sensational in tone, lacking in plot, and peopled by over-exaggerated characters of good or evil.

For myself, I believe the definition by Michael R. Booth in his study, *English Melodrama* (1965) comes closest to accurately defining the genre: 'Essentially, melodrama is a dream world inhabited by dream people and dream justice, offering audiences the fulfilment and satisfaction found only in dreams. An idealisation and simplification of the world of reality, it is in fact the world its audiences want but cannot get. In this world, life is uncomplicated, easy to understand, and immeasurably exciting. The world of melodrama is thus a world of certainties where confusion, doubt and perplexity are absent; a world of absolutes where after immense struggle and torment good triumphs over and punishes evil, and virtue receives tangible material rewards.'

In a nutshell, then, the melodrama provided its audiences with a diet of problems and disasters; although for the persecuted hero and tortured heroine, as well as the die-hard villain, there was only one inevitable outcome: good would always triumph over evil, no matter what the odds.

Melodramatic plays fell easily into two major categories: demonic and domestic. The first kind embraced all sorts of supernatural events and characters: devils, demons, vampires, ghosts and the like. The famous Gothic horror novels such as *The Castle of Otranto* by Horace Walpole (1764), Mrs Ann Radcliffe's *The Mysteries of Udolpho* (1794), and the notorious tale of the lecherous cleric, *The Monk* by Matthew Gregory Lewis (1796), had been the original inspiration for this type of production, and the plays drew heavily on their stock-in-trade locations such as ruined abbeys, moonlit churchyards, crumbling castles, haunted chambers, dark dungeons and so on. The plays all exploited the human emotion of 'fear-of-the-dark' and some of the characters were straight from nightmares, too. Of course, the demonic could on occasions stray into the domestic, but most theatre managements felt it was necessary to differentiate between the two to enable their audiences to be sure what they were getting. As a result, the two different categories developed.

The domestic melodrama dealt with real people in seemingly real situations — although the hero and heroine were probably far removed from the impoverished conditions of most of their audience. It was the emotions that were common to both, as Michael R. Booth has explained.

'Many domestic melodramas', he has written, 'do not have English settings and are at once removed from immediate reality.

Their emotions, sentiments and situations, however, are perfectly familiar.'

These domestic melodramas were as likely to be placed in an idyllic rural setting as a grim city background. Yet there would invariably be the villain of the piece in the shape of a hard-hearted squire or cruel landlord bent upon seduction, as well as the sorely tried hero and innocent heroine whose path to true love would be dogged by all the pitfalls of life. Crime was at the bottom of most of them — real crime, intended crime, or the crime associated in many people's minds with over-indulgence in drink, gambling or sex. At its most basic, the domestic melodrama utilised realistic raw materials processed into an end product of fantasy and wish fulfilment.

There were many real-life domestic crimes that made ideal material for the melodrama. A classic example was the story of Maria Marten, the molecatcher's daughter, who was seduced and murdered by the local squire, William Corder, in The Red Barn at Polstead in Suffolk in 1828. This drama, first recounted in the newspapers after Corder's arrest, trial and execution, soon became a long-running melodrama performed at all kinds of cheap theatres. It is still a favourite of repertory companies today.

Legendary figures like Robin Hood and Dick Turpin naturally co-mingled with more recent true stories, and all sorts of escapades — true, fictional and, frankly, sometimes unbelievable — were ascribed to them by the army of playwrights who kept the theatres supplied with scripts. As Maurice Wilson Disher says in *Blood and Thunder* (1949), his definitive study of Victorian melodrama and its origins, 'In cities where the increase in population was greatest, more theatres were needed, and more were provided with such enterprise that when Parliament freed the drama in 1843 (with the Licensing Act) the profession already had, what with the play-acting booths and saloons, all the freedom it needed. Blood and thunder flowed and rolled to the footlights everywhere.'

In the light of these facts, it is not difficult to understand why the story of *The String of Pearls* and, more particularly, the character of Sweeney Todd, should have been taken up by the theatre of melodrama. Nor, in truth, why the Demon Barber should soon become — and remain — one of the best-known characters in the theatre.

It was perhaps appropriate that the potential for adapting Thomas Prest's story for the stage should have first been appreciated by probably the greatest of all London's melodrama theatres, The Britannia in High Street, Hoxton. This was a theatre management for which Prest had produced material during the years 1841 to 1849 — a point to which I shall return shortly.

Today, unhappily, The Britannia is no more. But this former tavern which became one of the most popular cheap theatres of its time, has been immortalised in Charles Dickens's series of essays about London, *The Uncommercial Traveller*, published in 1861. Although, of course, with the passing of time, it is impossible to recreate the vanished playhouse — its flickering lights picking out the flamboyant gestures of the actors, and the noisy audiences shouting their cheers and boos between mouthfuls of beer and fried fish and potatoes — some mention of it is important. For this was, after all, where the greatest of all the monsters of melodrama, Sweeney Todd, first trod the boards.

Fortunately, something of the magic of the 'Brit' has been captured in print by Barton Baker, a regular visitor to the theatre, in his book, *The London Stage*, published in 1889:

'The Britannia — once called a saloon, but now a theatre — has only known one management, the founder, Sam Lane, and he has been succeeded by his widow, who still directs its destinies. Actors enter the theatre in their youth and remain there until age incapacitates them, or until they have strutted and fretted their last hour upon the stage of life. Authors wrote exclusively for this house, and it was the last to give up its own peculiar style of drama for second-hand West End pieces. Until very recently, its pantomimes enjoyed the longest runs in London, and are usually mounted with exceptional brilliancy.'

Hoxton High Street was itself a well-known centre for entertainment. Prior to the opening of the 'Brit', another hostelry, the Pimlico, where live entertainment was provided had stood on the same site for generations. The Britannia opened as a theatre on Easter Monday, 1841, offering, 'variety, grand concert, opera, vaudeville and laughable farce' with 'neither talent nor expense spared' at prices ranging from 6d (six pence) in the gallery to one shilling in the front stalls, 'with which a refreshment ticket is given'.

It was after the passing of the Licensing Act in 1843 that the 'Brit' turned to melodrama. So successful did this policy prove that in 1858 the old saloon was closed down and the premises were enlarged to form a colossal new theatre which could hold up to 5,000 people.

The names of just a few of the melodramas which the Britannia staged over the years are a clear indication as to why it could draw huge audiences from all over the metropolis: *The Mother's Dying Child, or Woman's Fate*; *Pure as Driven Snow, or Tempted in Vain*; *Taking The Veil* and *The Headless Horseman* to name just four. So it was surely with the usual sense of anticipation that the crowds streamed into the theatre on the night of 1 March, 1847 for the first performance of *The String of Pearls, or The Barber Fiend of Fleet Street*. Their interest may also have been heightened by the announcement below the title on the posters that the story was 'taken from the much admired Tale of that name in *Lloyd's People's Periodical*'; and even further whetted by the admission, 'For dramatic effect, and to adapt the story to general taste, some alterations have been judiciously made, enhancing its interest.'

Charles Dickens, who attended the 'Brit' on just such a night, has provided a graphic picture of the collection of noisy, colourful and uninhibited folk who made up a typical audience:

'We were a motley assemblage of people, and we had a good many boys and young men among us; we had also many girls and young women. To represent, however, that we did not include a very great number, and a very fair proportion of family groups, would be to make a gross mis-statement. Such groups were to be seen in all parts of the house. In the boxes and stalls particularly, they were composed of persons of very decent appearance, who had many children with them.

'Among our dresses there were most kinds of shabby and greasy wear, and much fustian and corduroy that was neither sound nor fragrant. The caps of our young men were mostly of the limp character, and we who wore them, slouched, high-shouldered, into our places with our hands in our pockets, and occasionally twisted our cravats about our necks like eels, and occasionally tied them down our breasts like links of sausages, and occasionally had a screw in our hair over each cheek bone with a slight thief-flavour in it.

'Besides prowlers and idlers, we were mechanics, dock-labourers, costermongers, petty tradesmen, small clerks, milliners, stay-makers, shoe-binders, shop workers, poor workers in a hundred highways and byways. Most of us — on the whole, the majority — were not at all clean, and not at all choice in our lives or conversation. But we had all come together in a place where our convenience was well consulted, and where we were well looked after, to enjoy an evening's entertainment in common. We were not going to loose any part of what we had paid for, through anybody's caprice, and as a community we had a character to lose. So, we were closely attentive, and kept excellent order. And let the man or boy who did otherwise instantly get out from this place, or we would put him out with the greatest expedition.'

The melodrama for that night of 1 March, *The String of Pearls*, was the handiwork of one of the theatre's busiest authors, George Dibdin Pitt, although he received no specific credit on the handbill. The fact that *The People's Periodical* was mentioned seems a clear indication that the serial had been popular with readers and the management were keen to associate their production with that success.

George Dibdin Pitt (1799–1855) came from a family who had been associated with the London theatre for many years, and while their fortunes appear to have varied from time to time, they were never long out of work or in financial need like a great many other people in the profession in the nineteenth century. George's mother was an actress and his father a song writer, and he naturally graduated into theatrical life when still a young man. He first tried acting with only modest success, then became a stage manager, before finally discovering his true métier as a playwright. His first drama was a piece entitled *My Own Blue Bell* performed at the Surrey Theatre in 1831.

The real upturn in Pitt's fortunes occurred in 1841 when Sam Lane took him on as the resident playwright at the newly opened Britannia. His skill at quickly devising melodramas around topics of interest seems to have already been well established — perhaps his biggest success having been *The Eddystone Elf*, a drama about a sea monster that haunts the famous lighthouse, produced at Sadler's Wells in 1834 — and within a very short time he was averaging at least one new play per month.

Like other dramatists providing material for the cheap theatres, Pitt got many of his plots from the penny journals — sometimes lifting stories virtually wholesale and making only minimal changes to the author's original dialogue. There was, as I have mentioned earlier, no copyright in operation then to prevent this piracy.

The many publications from Salisbury Square were rich sources of material, and there is evidence that writers like Thomas Prest sometimes offered their services to theatre owners in the hope of getting a little financial recompense from their tales rather than stand by and see them stolen for nothing. Indeed, we know that Prest had an agreement with Sam Lane during the 1840s, and it is my belief that he played a part in seeing *The String of Pearls* transferred to the stage, perhaps even lending George Dibdin Pitt a hand in the actual dramatisation. I base this belief on two things. Firstly, that the stage presentation of *The String of Pearls* opened on 1 March, *three weeks* before the serial reached its final episode in *The People's Periodical*; and although there are differences in the text of the serial and the play, the crucial closing episodes are much the same in both. These are surely developments that only Prest could have known and must have shared with Pitt — if he did not actually write some of the drama itself. Secondly — and here the evidence is more circumstantial — it is known that Pitt produced twenty-six plays during 1847: a total that even in those prolific days it seems hard to believe he could have achieved without some form of assistance. It therefore seems probable to me that Pitt and Prest pooled their talents on this occasion, too. The fact the play is not specifically credited to Pitt — as most of his other works were — is also a factor not without significance.

Although a copy of the playbill for the first performance of *The String of Pearls* is still in existence at the British Museum (and reproduced here), the names of the cast probably meant a great deal more to the patrons of the 'Brit' than they do to us today. However, they are worth mentioning because of their part in the launching of Sweeney Todd on the stage.

The Demon Barber himself was played by Mark Howard, who had starred as the villain in a number of melodramas, and was subsequently to become known as 'The Fiendish Figaro'. Indeed, Howard repeated the role several times during his career, and is credited with having originated a number of the manner-isms still associated with the part.

The role of Sweeney Todd's partner in crime, Mrs Lovett, was pioneered by a Miss Maria Hamilton, although it seems she did not retain the role for long. Most early recollections of the play state that the pie-maker was 'seductively played by Mrs Emma Atkinson', another familiar figure in melodrama at the time and the mother of the famous Sadler's Wells actress, Ann Atkinson. It was Mrs Lovett's fate to be shot by her paramour in this version, instead of either taking her own life or being poisoned.

Interestingly, too, the cruelly-wronged apprentice, Tobias Ragg, was actually played by a diminutive young woman, Mrs Hudson Kirby; while the part of the determined Colonel Jeffrey was taken by another of the 'Brit's' regular actors, Mr. J. Mor-daunt. Sam Sawford was the mysterious Jarvis Williams — revealed in the last scene to be the missing Mark Ingestre — with Miss C Braham as the beautiful Johanna Oakley.

These, then, were the players who gave the story of Sweeney Todd its first performance in March 1847, establishing a tradition that has continued to this day. Unfortunately, however, it was not the custom of the London theatre critics to attend productions at the Britannia — indeed, most tended to scorn all melodramas —

and only a single, eye-witness report has survived of an early production of the George Dibdin Pitt–Thomas Peckett Prest production. The account appears in Thomas W. Erle's book, *Letters From A Theatrical Scene Painter*, published in 1880. Evidence in the book suggests it must describe one of the earlier performances of the play, probably about 1850. I think it is well worth reprinting in full.

An evening at the Britannia during the run of 'The String of Pearls; *or,* The Barber Fiend of Fleet Street', *was to sup full of horrors. In the vulgar tongue of Hoxton and elsewhere, a full supper is called a 'tightener'. The expression is coarse, no doubt, yet suggestive. Abominably so. Going to see* The Barber Fiend *was a tightener of horrors, like a visit to the small room at Madame Tussaud's.*

The plot was as follows. The barber Fiend murders in succession all his customers who come to him to be shaved, and then, by way of utilising them to the utmost possible extent, as well as of conveniently disposing of their bodies, makes them into pies, upon which such of the characters as we are left to carry through the business of the piece, are regaled. A series of effects is produced by successive discoveries in the pies of what may be called 'internal evidence' of the true nature of their ingredients. Thus, one of the consumers finds in the first instance a woman's hair. This is not viewed as a circumstance of much gravity, since it is a matter of common experience that long hairs have an intrusive tendency which induces them to present themselves in combination with most alimentary substances. From buns, for example, they are as inseparable as grit.

But to return to the Barber's pies. The discovery of the hair is followed by that of a thumb nail, which appears to give rise to some indistinct, but uneasy, misgivings in the breast of the consumer. He pursues his meal with reflective hesitation, and with a zest which has now been obviously impaired by the operation of disquieting mental influences. The startling revelation of a brass button attached to a fragment of material substance of some kind or other which bears the aspect of having once formed a constituent portion of somebody or other's leather breeches, proves what is called 'a staggerer', and brings the repast to an abrupt and uncomfortable conclusion. The terrors of the scene culminate in the discovery of a full and detailed account of the whole matter set fourth on the paper in which the pies had been wrapped. The narrative in question is accompanied by strictures on the conduct of the murderer, ably drawn up by his victims, and a free and explicit confession by himself is also appended to the document. At this point a torrent of fiddles is let loose, which rasp away for some moments with an energy worthy of the crisis.

The Barber is then taken into custody. But not by policemen. Not a bit of it! The R B management knows better than that. Police constables, no doubt, constitute a highly respectable and estimable body of men. Still, when they march in with the mechanical precision of automata, as stiff as a procession of animated lamp-posts, and with countenances fraught with utter unmeaningness, they present, it must be confessed, the very essence of the unpicturesque in effect. And their plain, matter-of-fact truncheons are but silent and ineffective accessories to a situation. No. A party of supers rush in, attired in the uniforms in which they are acustomed to 'do' the Swedish army in Charles the Twelfth, and let off their muskets with signal intrepidity, firing earnestly upwards, as though anxious to hit some bird or other object which they must be supposed to have descried flitting about up among the gas patterns. This light fusillade, incidentally, brings about the desirable result of creating a strong smell of gunpowder, and the noise throws a collection of urchins at the door of the theatre, who cannot muster their sixpence for the gallery, into paroxysms of excitement to know what is going on inside. Of all the various sad forms of human destitution, perhaps the most affecting to contemplate is that of small boys who hang night after night about the doors of theatres but can't afford to go in.

The apprehension of the wicked barber necessarily brings the drama to its conclusion, and at this point, therefore, all the

*murdered characters reappear. If it be objected that the suppo-
sition of his guilt is weakened by, not to say is absolutely
inconsistent with, the bodily presence of his victims — the*
ipsissima corpora delictorum *— all as right and tight as
can be, the answer is that the claims of the final tableau
are paramount. The scene is illuminated with red fire. An
explanation of the propriety of this enrichment of the tableau
is probably to be sought in the notion of its being in some
degree typical of the subject-matter of the piece, since it is not
within ordinary experience that the action of retributive justice
is attended by any such meteoric phenomena. The whole of
the characters then joined in a patriotic song, in which the
invasion panic, and the discomfiture of the enemy by the gal-
lantry of the Hoxton volunteers, together with any other points
which may happen to be of general interest to the community
at that particular moment, are very neatly and happily touched
off.*

*Now if that isn't a 'strong' piece, pray what is? If the reader
does not agree with me in so characterising it, I should then
be glad to be put in possession of his views as to what is a
strong piece. Surely the conversion of one half of the characters
in the drama into animal sustenance for the other half is an
incident of a complexion sufficiently decided to arrest attention.
In the ultimate dénouement of the plot more formidable and
perplexing difficulties have to be encountered than even in the
case of a certain novel which was published in parts in one of
the penny awfuls some time ago. In that instance, the author,
on getting into a tiff with the editor of the periodica, brought
the story which was in course of publication to an abrupt and
absurd conclusion by taking all his characters out in a boat to
a spot about midway between Dover and Calais, and there
upsetting them into the sea, and drowning them like a litter
of mongrel puppies. Subsequently, however, being desirous to
publish his work in a separate form on his own account, he
became obliged to fish them all up again from the bottom of
the sea, and set them to work out a proper conclusion as best
they might. But in* **The Barber Fiend** *half the dramatis per-*

sonae have to be resuscitated after mastication and digestion by the other half.

I must say the Barber was well played and as dramatic impressions are so strong with me, I should not go out of my way to get my hair cut in Fleet Street just at present. The uncomfortable atmosphere of suspicion and distrust which already envelops the rations of opaque slime and gristle conventionally known as mutton pies is amply sufficient of itself, without the addition of any further unpleasant misgivings which might be suggested by **The Barber Fiend**, to discourage one from partaking of those ambiguous delicacies. When I was at school, a man who sold mutton pies to the boys went the way of all piemen, and his son succeeded to the business. It was currently reported and believed that **no funeral ever took place**. This, under the circumstances, was a tremendous fact. For it afforded room for surmising that the expression that the deceased had 'gone the way of all flesh' was pregnant with unusual significance. If it had been stated that he had 'gone to his last home', his place of final rest and his son's mutton pies, might, not impossibly, under the particular conditions of his disappearance, have proved to be convertible terms.

It was a disappointment that there was no call for the author, as I should have liked to have seen the party. His cast of mind must be a sort of combination of Lady Macbeth's with that of the editor of **The Newgate Calendar** *[sic]*. He must reside in some spectral and gloomy scene, such as Gower Street, or the immediate vicinity of Cold Bath Field's Prison, where the picture of desolate and dreary waste which is ever presented to his view is unrelieved by any stray gleam of a cheerful tint. Moreover, the conception and composition of **The Barber Fiend** must have taken place in his moments of acute indigestion. Perverted fancies of the imagination like this are usually the result of functional disorder in the system.

Joking apart, I think that the representation of such a mass of unnatural and repulsive horrors is extremely wrong and pernicious, and the subsequent astonishing resuscitation of the victims does little to rectify it. If the Drama be 'holding *the mirror up to nature', it should also be remembered that there is such a thing, and a very real and common thing too, as holding nature up to the mirror. For the contemplation, or vivid description, of an art of wickedness, frequently, as is perfectly known, inoculates weak minds with an irresistible impulse to do the same kind of thing. It was in this course that Courvoisier, who murdered his master, Lord William Russell, declared himself to have been brought to the gallows, and there have been many similar instances. Besides which, it isn't the pleasantest thing in the world to sit for an hour or two looking at murders, although they are but sham ones, nor is it in good taste to have too many of them on the stage.*

It is doubtful whether the majority of the first night audience of *The String of Pearls* as they poured noisily out of the theatre shared Thomas Erle's reservations about the play. They were, after all, in the main people who were hardened to tales of crime and death, who enjoyed descriptions of murder and killings, and could take violence and passion in their stride. They may not have had Erle's sensibilities, either, but they would have agreed that the idea of a drama about a man who murdered his customers and turned them into meat pies was definitely unusual: certainly something to make you think twice the next time you decided to visit a barber or buy a tasty meat pie!

Perhaps, too, there were some members of the audience that night — and in the nights to come — who might have remembered the story of the original 'Barber Fiend of Fleet Street' which had been a part of London gossip for half a century. Indeed, prominently printed on the bills outside the theatre — just beneath the title of the play — were the words, FOUNDED ON FACT. But no matter how many saw that statement, or even bothered to consider whether it was intended as some sort of justification for the horrors, Thomas Erle's protest that putting on such a story was 'wrong and pernicious' fell on deaf ears. The Demon Barber had now made his bow in literature and in the theatre and would never be removed from centre stage again.

15

Idol of the Rogues' Gallery

By the end of the nineteenth century, Sweeney Todd was a firmly established favourite in print and on the stage. The life and crimes of the Demon Barber had been novelised and serialised several times more, all the versions drawing heavily on Thomas Prest's *The String of Pearls*; while the Britannia's theatrical version had been similarly appropriated by other places of entertainment. As Maurice Disher has written in *Blood and Thunder*, 'Henceforward, Sweeney Todd would rank in the rogue's gallery of the sensation-loving public as second only to that perpetual idol of the nineteenth-century masses, Dick Turpin.'

There was clearly something about Sweeney Todd which struck a chord with audiences, and he became the 'villain you love to hate' in print and on the stage. Aside from the public's mixture of fascination and revulsion at the hints of cannibalism, the Demon Barber's notoriety was no doubt helped by the timing of his appearance when novels and plays were cross-fertilising each other to a very considerable extent. As Wilkie Collins expressed it in a preface to his novel, *Basil* (1852): 'The novel and the play are twin-sisters in the family of Fiction: the one is a drama narrated, as the other is a drama acted. All the strong and deep emotions that the playwright is privileged to excite, the novelist is privileged to excite also.' This view is also shared by a modern commentator, Richard D. Altick in his book, *Victorian Studies in Scarlet* (1972), where he writes, 'Such is probably the case with the most memorable of the horrific stories that became part of Victorian popular lore — the tale of Sweeney

Todd, the mad barber of Fleet Street, whose penny shaving shop was equipped with a trapdoor beside [sic] the barber chair.'

The number of emphemeral publications and little theatre versions of Todd's story which were produced during the Victorian era will probably never be known. Certainly the British Museum has very few copies, and in some instances only the titles of the stories and plays have survived at all. Commenting on this, Montague Summers wrote in *A Gothic Bibliography*, 'There have been innumerable melodramatic adaptations of Sweeney Todd, many of which were never printed and only hastily made for the very minor theatres. Nonetheless, in one or other of the adaptations, the play has been frequently played in London and throughout the provinces ever since.'

As Summers suggests, what all these productions served to achieve was the continuing fame of Sweeney Todd.

The original stage production of *The String of Pearls* at the Britannia certainly continued for some years — alternating with both new melodramas and revivals of some of the old favourites. It was also revised several times to highlight the villainy of Sweeney Todd and remove some of the extraneous characters who cluttered up the original. It was, after all, the Fiend of Fleet Street that the paying public at the 'Brit' came to see.

Some later versions of the story included a bibulous clergyman bent on seduction; a large Beefeater from the Tower of London given to roars of hearty laughter at inappropriate moments; and a clutch of comic policemen. A further alteration in 1860 had the villain being foiled not by a hero, but by the principal comedian — a device which has subsequently been worked to death by other playwrights.

As the century drew to a close, Sweeney Todd even began to appear as a character in other plays, too. Sometimes he was just a subsidiary villain, introduced as a crowd-puller when the mere mention of his name was enough to guarantee boos and hisses from the audience; while in a number of the cheaper travelling shows and 'penny gaffs' he remained a star in his own right — though he was often attributed with even more horrendous crimes than either real life, Prest or Pitt had attributed to him.

A souvenir booklet sold at public performances of Sweeney Todd,
The Demon Barber *throughout Britain at the turn of the century.*

Probably the next major stageplay to feature his activities was produced by Frederick Hazelton in 1862. It is clear from the title that the author had his priorities right and knew exactly who the public were coming to see. *Sweeney Todd, the Barber of Fleet Street*, he called his version, adding: *or, The String of Pearls*.

Hazelton's new melodrama was in three acts and actually began where the other stories left off with Todd being arrested outside his shop and conveyed to Newgate. From here he escapes intent on murdering Mrs Lovett whom he believes has informed on him to the authorities. The play was climaxed by a fight between the pair which ended with the Demon Barber falling through his own trapdoor and being consumed by flames. The production was first staged at the Bower Saloon in Lambeth and ran there successfully for some time before its transfer to the Pavillion Theatre in Mile End. The man who played Sweeney Todd in this production was George Yates whose performance was compared to that of Mark Howard. A critic, Henry C. Porter, writing in 1902, said 'Yates took the part of the Barber Fiend, and made it very popular among the patrons of the fourth-rate playhouses.' A recent historian, Michael Kilgarrif in his *Golden Age of Melodrama* (1974) adds further: 'The most celebrated Demon Barber of the century was George Yates of the Pavillion, Mile End, who, with his large-sized wife, Harriet Clifton, as Mrs Lovett, made as fearsome a duo as a horror addict could wish for in a month of Bloody Sundays.'

Another actor who made something of a speciality of the role of Sweeney Todd was Cecil Pitt, who had appeared in a minor role as the keeper of a madhouse in the first production at the Britannia. He was actually the younger brother of George Dibdin Pitt and so may well have been able to claim a special inside knowledge of the part. Cecil Pitt also appeared as Todd in another version of the story written by Matt Wilkinson which, although it again followed Thomas Peckett Prest's original story-line, made more of the Demon Barber as an evil seducer of young girls. Daringly, for its time, it had Todd leching after his assistant 'Charley Green', apparently unaware that the 'boy' was actually the beautiful Johanna Oakley in disguise.

It was not until this century, however, that the actor whose name is still most closely associated with the role of Sweeney Todd first played the role on the stage and then succesfully transplanted the Demon Barber to film. His name was, appropriately, Tod Slaughter.

Slaughter, the 'master of melodrama' as he is remembered, probably did more than anyone to bridge Sweeney Todd's fame from the Victorian era to recent times. His name became synonymous with the role, and when he died in February 1956 it was claimed that he had appeared in the part over 4,000 times on the stage, as well as in the classic screen version, in a career that spanned over fifty years.

* * *

It is a popular misconception that Tod Slaughter was the first person to play the Demon Barber on film in 1936. This is not, in fact, the case: Sweeney Todd made his début on the screen during the silent era in a comedy burlesque made by New Era Films in 1926. Called simply *Sweeney Todd*, this short, silent movie bore more similarity to a Keystone Cops farce than the grisly tale of the Fleet Street murderer. It was ostensibly based on George Dibdin Pitt's play, but the screenwriter, P. L. Mannock took quite a few liberties with the story, while the director, George Dewhurst played most of the action for laughs. The only actor credited in the picture is G. A. Baughan who appeared as Sweeney Todd. The film was apparently premiered at the unlikely venue of the Cinematograph Garden Party in 1926! Sadly, no copy appears to have survived.

The second picture, made two years later by Stoll Films, was a much more substantial effort, and the uncredited scriptwriter drew on the work of both Pitt and Frederick Hazelton, although his version did vary in one significant way. Initially, the writer stuck to the theme of the Demon Barber who slits the throats of his customers, steals their valuables and then throws the bodies into a cellar where they are collected by the widow Lovett for making into pies for her cooked meat shop next door. But instead of being arrested and executed for his crimes, this Sweeney Todd — played by Moore Marriott —awakes in his bed to find the whole thing has been a bad dream.

The reason for this *volte farce* has never been satisfactorily explained. Did the producer, Harry Rowson, feel the original story was too much for sensitive stomachs in the twenties? Or were Stoll Films afraid that the subject matter might prove too revolting for the public who were then just getting over reading the horrific details of the arrest and trial of Fritz Hartman, a German homosexual killer, who had murdered some fifty young men and boys between 1918 and 1924 and sold their flesh for human consumption in his cooked meat shop? Whatever the reason, Moore Marriott nevertheless made quite a success of his role, although he is, of course, better remembered for playing the hoary old rustic in the Will Hay comedies of the thirties and forties. His co-stars were Zoe Palmer and Charles Ashton as the hero and heroine, Johanna Oakley and Mark Ingestre.

It is, however, the Tod Slaughter version of *Sweeney Todd, The Demon Barber of Fleet Street*, made with sound and in black and white by Ambassador Pictures in 1936, that remains the best known movie to date.

Tod Slaughter had, as I mentioned earlier, been playing the role for many years in theatres throughout the British Isles, but the movie directed by the versatile George King assured him of a place in the ranks of the cinema's great horror stars.

Seeing the picture today, Tod Slaughter can easily be accused of an over-the-top performance; but there is no denying the ghoulish relish with which he tackles the role, nor the fact that the picture has now become a cult classic — particularly in America where it is favourite on college campuses and at film festivals. In this version, the scriptwriters, Frederick Hayward and H. F. Maltby, took George Dibdin Pitt's play as their starting point; but made a great deal more of the razor-slashing, throat-cutting and human pie-making ⅋lements of the tale than anyone before them had done. Tod Slaughter, for his part, was said to have become so immersed in the role that he genuinely frightened some of his fellow actors when they had to sit in the revolving chair. A youthful Bruce Seton played Mark Ingestre, with Eve Lister as Johanna and Stella Rho as a malevolent Mrs Lovett.

Like Basil Rathbone as Sherlock Holmes, Tod Slaughter was destined thereafter to be forever associated with the part of Sweeney Todd — although he could well claim to have established the Demon Barber in yet another medium of entertainment.

The actor was born Norman Carter Slaughter in Newcastle-upon-Tyne in 1885, and his road to stardom had been a long and hard one. Beginning with walk-on parts, followed by small roles in provincial rep, it was not for some years that he realised that his talent lay in playing villains, especially in revivals of the old melodramas.

Slaughter established his reputation in the years immediately after the First World War when he took over as actor-manager of the old Elephant & Castle Theatre in London, and there staged a whole series of blood and thunder melodramas including *The Murder in the Red Barn, Jack Sheppard, Spring Heeled Jack* and, of course, *Sweeney Todd*. He repeated a number of these roles in both radio and film adaptations which brought his name to an even wider audience.

After the Second World War, Tod Slaughter continued to be a popular box office draw at theatres throughout the country, starring in a number of Grand Guignol plays, of which *Sweeney Todd* remained far and away the most successful. According to his friends, he was a demon for work — indeed he listed his hobbies in *Who's Who* as 'gardening and work' — and continued to appear on stage right up to the time of his death. Sadly, although he enjoyed a long and happy marriage to the actress Jenny Lind (whom he had 'slain' in virtually every conceivable manner during their stage partnership), he was rather less successful in running his financial affairs, and three years before his death a receiving order for bankruptcy was issued against him.

'After fifty years in the theatre,' he said ruefully after the court hearing, 'with a completely clean record, this is *humiliating*.'

When Tod Slaughter died on 19 February, 1956, the press had certainly not forgotten his glory days. The *Daily Mail*, for instance, spread the news across three columns under the heading THE SMILING VILLAIN NOBODY CONDEMNED, while even *The Times* subtitled its obituary, 'The Demon Barber of the Stage'. The *Mail's* entertainment writer, Cecil Wilson, expressed the feelings of millions when he wrote:

'Tod Slaughter, the most lovable multi-murderer on the British stage, the villain with the comedian's face, who immortalised the crimes of Sweeney Todd, the Demon Barber, died in his sleep yesterday. He had appeared in *The Murder in the Red Barn* on Saturday night. The man who, in private life, could not bring himself to strangle a chicken, would have been 71 next month, and murder most foul has been his speciality for most of his 51 years in the theatre.

'He had 340 plays in his repertoire — mostly gruesome affairs in which the villain was always of the blackest, the hero the noblest, and the heroine the sweetest — and he was always the grateful target for every boo and hiss.'

The *News Chronicle* headlined its report DEMON BARBER WAS LAST OF HIS KIND, and said, 'Over four thousand times as Sweeney Todd he severed jugulars and brought horror to the faces of his audiences as rich-red cochineal spurted from his property razor. Many people in and out of the theatre called him Sweeney because he was so identified with the role.'

The appropriately named John Barber of the *Daily Express* — who also happened to be a friend of the performer — declared 'no living actor curdled more blood or stormed more barns than Norman Carter Slaughter'.

He continued: 'His flickering eyebrows and throaty chuckle had gloated over red ketchup spouting from countless jugulars. His unforgettable cry, "Oh, I'd love to polish you off!" addressed to interrupters on average 12 times a performance, six nights a week, made him a legend long before his death.

'Yet he was an artist. He did not just rant through a blood-stained repertoire. No one was quicker to sense an audience's mood. When he carved, he cut clean and sure with a gleaming knife. I can still hear him, as he stepped across the road to the theatre, "Coming in, John? I'm killing them well in the oven tonight!" '

Posthumously, Tod Slaughter's fame is growing once more and his films are receiving fresh critical attention. A clearer impression of his contribution to entertainment is also emerging, as the *Daily Mail* has stated:

'For all his dastardly deeds on the stage, there were no outcrys in his heyday about the sinister influence of Tod Slaughter on the youth of Britain. Perhaps it was because his plays remained such a safe distance from reality. "The best children have a natural taste for the horrific," he once said. "Their games deal mostly with killing, and it is a wholesome way of letting off steam." '

It was thanks in no small degree to Tod Slaughter's contribution that Sweeney Todd has remained one of the most popular figures in drama. The actor's own mantle has been taken on by Glasgow-born Elliott Williams, who calls himself 'The Last of the Barnstormers', and has been playing the Demon Barber as part of his repertoire for the last forty years. His annual performances in the Wax Museum at the Edingburgh Festival Fringe are always one of the highlights of the show.

As far as the various plays about Sweeney Todd are concerned, they remain among the most popular of any performed by either amateur or professional companies. Indeed, each year they are put on hundreds of times by groups all over the world according to Samuel French Ltd of London who control the copyright in three of the most popular versions written by Christopher Bond, Austin Rosser and Brian J. Burton respectively. A spokesman for the company told me that the story of Sweeney Todd was probably, year in and year out, the most successful on their entire list.

These more recent versions of the story play it much straighter, with elements of pathos and comedy as well as the blood and thunder. In Christopher Bond's version, for example, there is an attempt to win some sympathy for Todd by portraying him as a man who has been cruelly wronged by society and succumbed to the deadly attraction of holding the life and death of others in the grip of his palm.

Apart from countless amateur and repertory players, the role of Sweeney Todd has been played by a number of our leading actors including John Lawson, Donald Britton, Brian Murphy and Gordon Jackson, the latter famous for his part as the punctilious butler, Hudson, in TV's *Upstairs, Downstairs*.

The flamboyant Freddie Jones was the first man to play the Demon Barber on television in ABC's successful series, *Mystery and Imagination*, which ran from 1965 to 1970. The hour-long adaptation of the story was scripted by Vincent Tilsley who subtitled the story, 'The Daydreamer in the Dark' and concentrated on the struggle between Todd's conscience and his greed for money and influence. Freddie Jones's lip-smacking, eye-rolling, blood-thirsty performance was well supported by a juicy Heather Canning as Mrs Lovett.

The great comedian Stanley Holloway recorded a monologue about the Demon Barber which has subsequently become a favourite on many radio request programmes. BBC Radio has also broadcast a number of plays featuring Sweeney Todd, with the J. P. Quaine version, first heard in 1932, one of the most widely praised.

Indeed, in the intervening years, the Dermon Barber has appeared in one unlikely place after another: as part of a routine by Bud Flanagan in the Crazy Gang shows; in novels such as B. L. Farjeon's *Devlin The Barber* (1963) and short stories like 'Speciality of the House' by Stanley Ellin and 'Free Dirt' by Charles Beaumont; not to mention children's comics where he cropped up in the fifties in *The Rover* as 'The Demon Barber' and as an unlikely comic strip character 'Sweeney Toddler' in *Whoopee* in the seventies.

The universal appeal of Sweeney Todd's name is to be found virtually everywhere. He is sometimes encountered as the star of fairground horror shows — like The Haunted House where he slashes at screaming couples in a huge revolving chair — and his soubriquet is often given to barbers and pie shops in these less squeamish times.

He crops up in the newspapers, too, particularly in any items to do with hairdressing. In July 1949, for instance, during a discussion of the Hairdresser's bill in the House of Commons, he was actually cited by an MP during his address to members. The bill was an attempt to make registration a requirement for anyone practising as a hairdresser in order to ensure higher standards in the trade. While speaking about a weakness in the proposed law, John Paton, the Labour MP for Norwich said, 'Under the provisions of the bill, Sweeney Todd, the Demon Barber of Fleet Street, could go on for the rest of his life not only shaving throats, but cutting them, provided he always remembered to pay his annual registration fee.' The bill was rejected by 67 votes to 53.

Perhaps, though, the most curious use of the barber's name has been as Cockney rhyming slang for Scotland Yard's Flying Squad. Known as 'The Sweeney', these elite members of the police force have an enviable reputation for catching the most vicious criminals and hardened villains. *The Sweeney* was also, of course, the name of a television series that ran from 1974 to 1978 starring John Thaw and Dennis Waterman.

In 1979, the whole legend leapt back into the general public's consciousness once more with the news that the outstanding American composer Stephen Sondheim had written a 'Musical-Thriller' version of the story staring Len Cariou as Todd and Angela Lansbury as Mrs Lovett. Spectacularly staged at the Uris Theatre, New York as a kind of black-comedy opera, the production had been adapted by Hugh Wheeler from the script of English playwright Christopher Bond, and was directed by Harold Prince with all the panache for which he is famous. It was a most suitable play to be in the hands of the man known as 'The Demon King of Broadway'. However, unlike the very earliest productions in the Victorian 'penny gaffs' which had cost mere pounds to stage, this extravaganza was said to have been capitalised at just under one million dollars.

In Sondheim's Sweeney Todd, the barber has become a victim of injustice. Sentenced to transportation to Australia by a lecherous judge who covets his wife, Todd manages to escape on the journey and returns to London where he finds his spouse a virtual madwoman. He vows to be revenged, and with the aid of a neighbour, Mrs Lovett, who has preserved his razors during his absence, the pair begin their muderous operations.

This Sweeney Todd was notable for having a minimum of spoken narrative and some twenty-six musical numbers of which the bitter-sweet ballads 'Pretty Woman' and 'Johanna' plus the sardonic 'A Little Priest' about meat pies, and Sweeney Todd's big song, 'Epiphany' were outstanding. There are, indeed, some critics who have described this 'ballad opera' as the forerunner of a number of the lavish musicals which are now being played to full houses all around the world. The influence of Sweeney Todd, it would seem, has struck again!

Aside from excellent reviews, the American production also won eight Tony awards, two Grammy awards, and was named Best Musical of 1979 by the New York Critics' Circle. RKO also filmed a multi-camera version of the stage show for screening on TV.

In 1980, the play transferred to London and The Theatre Royal, Drury Lane where it was heralded as 'Britain's most expensive musical ever' (at £500,000) with Denis Quilley and Sheila Hancock in the leading roles. The choice of Sheila as Mrs Lovett provided a curious family connection, as her husband John Thaw later explained: 'It's funny that I was in *The Sweeney* for so long — I never thought Sheila would pick up the name when I'd finished with it!' Such was the interest in this production that London Weekend Television devoted their South Bank Show hosted by Melvyn Bragg to the mounting of the show and a look at the legend of Sweeney Todd. Much of my original research was embodied into the programme.

What I personally found most satisfying about the musical was its attempt to recreate the London in which Sweeney Todd had lived. Indeed, looking at the complex scenery of decaying buildings, iron structures and sulphureously smoking chimneys, was almost a case of *déjà vu* — reminding me of what I had seen in my mind's eye all those years earlier when I had first started to research the story. Irving Wardle put it all neatly into words in his review for *The Times*:

'London is presented as a vision of hell peopled with ragged madwomen, asylum directors, corrupt officials and a populace gorging themselves on the tasty dishes that Sweeney Todd and Mrs Lovett make. The show rivets you to your seat, freezes your blood, and leaves you with the feeling that the Demon Barber is alive and well and sitting all around you in Drury Lane.'

For some critics, like Robert Cushman of the *Observer*, 'the show touched greatness,' and he saw echoes from the past when audiences 'listened raptly and cheered at the end'. Michael Billington in the *Guardian* added his own words of praise — along with a striking example of presentiment. 'There is no denying,' he wrote, 'that Sondheim and Prince have conceived a remarkable Brechtian barber's opera and totally transformed an antique melodrama. It is a brilliant piece of musical theatre; a dense, complex, thorough-composed work that would not have disgraced (indeed would have enhanced) the stages of opera houses throughout the world. I am convinced that, like most of Stephen Sondheim's work, it will have a life beyond its immediate run.'

Prophetic words indeed. For though both the American and British productions of the musical did not last as long as expected back in the early eighties, now, like the Demon Barber himself, the musical is set to be revived this autumn. There is talk, too, of a film version of the story to be made by Tim Burton, the superlative director of Batman and Edward Scissorhands.

The gruesome murderer who went to his end on the gallows at Newgate almost two hundred years ago has now found a fame far beyond that of almost any other criminal. His famous catch-phrase is surely destined to ring out for many a year to come: 'Oh, how I love to polish 'em off!'

One of many recent pictures of the infamous barber of Fleet Street
– by Cliff Edwards in the 'Hair Raisers' series.

AFTERWORD

Since the first publication of this book in London in 1993, interest in the legend of Sweeney Todd has increased fourfold. Stephen Sondheim's musical, *Sweeney Todd*, returned three years on for a new run at the Haymarket in London's Leicester Square starring Dave Willetts and Jeanette Ranger as Todd and Mrs Lovett. Both had previously been stars of the phenomenally successful *Les Miserables* and planned to take the show on to New York

Neil Gaiman, the highly regarded scripter of SF comics and graphic novels, has also produced an illustrated version of the story with Michael Zulli called *Sweeney Todd 'Penny Dreadful'*. This limited edition work, now much sought-after by collectors, carried the warning, 'Those who create unauthorised and unlawful reprints will be served up piping hot at Mrs Lovett's in Bell Yard.' Cliff Edwards and Michael Strand have similarly retold the legend in the 'Hair Raisers' series of illustrated paperbacks produced especially for younger readers by Longmans.

London and the Home Counties now boast a number of business premises named after the Barber of Fleet Street – including at least a dozen hairdressers, several bakers' shops and a very popular hostelry in the heart of London in Tooley Street. Only Fleet Street still awaits a memento of its most villainous resident. In this context, a short while ago I was told a story by a former Fleet Street journalist concerning a visit he made to a hairdresser's not a stone's throw from Temple Bar.

'As I sat in the chair awaiting a shave,' the journalist recalled, 'the barber carefully sharpened his razor and then brandished it in front of my eyes. Just as he was about to apply it to my soap-covered face, he suddenly remarked, "Death seems far away on a beautiful morning like this." I looked uneasily around, wondering why he should have said this. There was no one else in the shop. It was almost as sinister as Sweeney Todd's famous, "I polish 'em off!" Thereafter I christened the barber (who was a Scandinavian), "Sven Todd". He did not appear to see the joke himself. Nor did I – till I had left his shop!'

Recently, prints of the original film of Sweeney Todd starring Tod Slaughter have been painstakingly restored and screened at a number of film clubs and on late night television. As I write this, a big-budget new movie version has been directed by John Schlesinger (of *Midnight Cowboy* fame) starring Ben Kingsley and Joanna Lumley in the lead roles. One London newspaper columnist writing about the filming warned Ben Kingsley he had a difficult act to follow as Tod Slaughter was a contender for the title off 'the second hammiest British actor ever, after Sir Donald Wolfit.'

Research into the legend has also continued among historians and writers specialising in London subjects, with the most recent contributions appearing in the *Illustrated London News*, the *Independent* and *The Times*. Sweeney Todd may well have been dead almost two hundred years but his notoriety is, if anything, even stronger. And I cannot help feeling that perhaps even stranger developments may emerge in the third century of the 'Demon Barber's' fame!

PETER HAINING,
February 1998

Neil Gaiman's menacing picture of the serial murderer from his book, Sweeney Todd, The Demon Barber of Fleet Street.